BURGLARY

A VERY PERSONAL CRIME

by

Detective Jon M. Robert
Miami-Dade Police Department Retired

Introduction

CHAPTER EIGHT
Things to Consider

CHAPTER NINE
If You Become a Victim

In Conclusion

Training / Certifications

Awards / Commendations

"Your most powerful skills (weapons) are psychological ones; patience, tolerance, tact, good humor and the ability to set an example by your own conduct."

"People don't listen to what you say, they watch what you do. More importantly, they remember how you made them feel."

Author Unknown

DEDICATION

To my loving wife Michelle, who stood by me through the countless days and nights while I was in the field conducting investigations. It takes a remarkable woman, a very special woman, to be the wife of a police officer. Without her love and support I would not have been half the person then or now. I love you "My Baby".

Also, I would be remiss not to thank our entire family, to include our law enforcement family, whom supported me with love and prayers. They are all warriors for the cause.

Thanks to Kim Menkhorst. Kim started out as my realtor and turned out to be a blessing in the marketing and development of this book.

Also, to some very special friends, David and Susan Teich and Denise Ducote. Their contribution both independently and collectively to the development of this book is beyond comprehension.

And finally, to the many victims for which I had the honor of serving.

INTRODUCTION

So here it goes… First, I want to let you know that in the police academy we were told that over the course of our career we would write more in the form of police reports than most award-winning novelists. That statement rang very true over my twenty-nine-year career with the Miami-Dade Police Department in Miami, Florida and the City of Gainesville Police Department in Gainesville, Florida. Ironically, I now find myself writing this book. My wish is to talk to you (the reader) via my written words, just as I connected with the victims, I had the honor of serving.

All in all, I spent the majority of my career specializing in burglary investigations. After thousands of investigations and a countless number of interviews/interrogations of burglars, I realized an opportunity and need for change.

As an investigator I experienced early on somewhat of an awakening to the crime of burglary. This came from witnessing victim after victim expressing themselves in ways that did not and never would compare to any number of other so-called "property crimes". I watched as victims expressed feelings of anger and/or sadness as I sat with them in their homes after having suffered a burglary. Many cried in disbelief. I held crying children immediately following an in-progress burglary whom had been traumatized by a burglar who had entered the home while mother/father were at work. Children that had been taught to never answer a knock at the door when home alone.

I dealt with countless victims of burglary and quickly came to the realization that the crime of burglary was much more complex and wasn't a mere "property crime" as it is typically classified by many police departments and prosecuted by many State's Attorney's. A crime whereby you simply file a police report, report what was stolen and file a claim with your insurance company. No! This is a crime that was a personal attack on its victims! The majority of victims I dealt with realized only too late how profound of a crime. Time and time again victims would say, "If only I had known".

Whether my victims were young or old, male or female, I found all were personally affected. Perhaps one of the most devastating effects of becoming the victim of a residential burglary is psychological. Many victims expressed to me feelings of fear, insecurity, anxiety, depression and even the feeling of having been violated. All of these feelings and emotions often bring with it a myriad of other serious and debilitating effects. Some endured sleepless nights; many women felt the need to discard their personal clothing items knowing that these items had been touched by a complete stranger; children experienced nightmares fearing that the boogie man would return and there were those who sought professional help in order to better cope with the crime.

Of course, beyond the personal and psychological effects victims deal with the theft and/or destruction of property. Burglars kick in doors, break windows, throw furnishings about and any number of other damaging acts in the process of gaining entry to your home or business. In a matter of minutes if not seconds a burglar will destroy and steal what took years for you to acquire.

Another commonality to burglary is the story a victim tells as to the theft of a particular item. Take jewelry for example. Whether male or female, jewelry always tells a story. Whether the jewelry was self-purchased, gifted or inherited it has special meaning and recalls memories. I'm sure that right now you can think of a number of your own memories as your reading this. The impact of this type of loss harkens back to the personal effect of this crime. It's not just about the intrinsic value of the item, it's a sentimental claim that can never be recovered.

In this book I hope to take you on a journey of insight into the world of burglary and the mindset of the burglar with which you will glean all that I learned and experienced. I plan to cover a multitude of topics ranging from: awareness and prevention, inventory, insurance, having a gun in your home or business, education and having a plan. I will also talk about issues such as opening your home to guests, your children and their friends, pets, parties, cleaning services and contractors. Along the way I will include stories of cases that I handled which I feel have pertinence to a particular topic or those which support further just how personally the crime of burglary effects it's victims. I also snuck in a few random "quick notes" and lighthearted memories. So, let's begin.

CHAPTER ONE

*C*HANGING THE FACE OF THE CRIME

The goal is to ***Change the Face of the Crime.***

I coined the phrase *change the face of the crime* as it seemed appropriate in not only defining the goal, change, though also the peripheral elements of burglary, or what I refer to as, the face.

In researching what elements of burglary were most intrinsic to the crime I decided to address quite a number of issues, all of which are listed in the outline of this book. As it turned out there was a plethora of topics to cover.

Flashback

I just had a flashback to the time when I first ever heard the word plethora. I was working uniform patrol as a young officer and the Platoon Commander (you know who you are) entered the Roll Call room. Now this Commander was of Cuban descent and spoke with a Spanish accent, English being his second language, though he prided himself in mastering the English language. He had one of those "word of the day" dictionaries and didn't miss a day. He also kept himself in stellar shape as he enjoyed working out on a regular basis. You know what I'm talking about. Anyway, getting back to the flashback... he stood at the head of the squad and his instruction was to, 'go out there today and write a plethora of tickets'. I'll never forget half the squad looking inquisitively at each other. One officer retrieved a pocket dictionary from his report case. I'll never forget that moment or the Commander who was one of the best in the Department and to him, I say thank you.

I next had to decide how best to convey my message. Given my years of experience and knowledge of the crime I knew that it wasn't about creating a list of instructions that may or may not apply to any one person. After thinking long and hard I decided that the best approach would be to bring awareness to each of the elements connected to the crime. My belief is that through awareness one can develop his or her own resolve to prevention and create a more personal approach to the goal.

As is true in so many cases, awareness is key. I love using the word aware. Most dictionaries define awareness as having knowledge and/or consciousness. Throughout my career I found that being aware was key to many, if not all, aspects of police work. From day one out of the police academy as a rookie I was instructed to be aware and I continued to pass that along later as a Field Training Officer instructing new officers assigned to uniform patrol. I think all of us can agree that absent awareness, one would be somewhat lost in this world we live in.

Burglary is a crime that devastates victims monetarily on the surface and more importantly personally in their heart and mind. I know that by the time you finish reading this book you will have gained a newfound awareness to this very personal crime and gained the knowledge to effectively make changes to your home or business to protect you and your family for years to come.

There is a bizarre commonality between these crimes and the people committing them. It's almost as if all burglars have attended the same school of burglary and thus each are following the same methods and behavior. So, why could we not utilize these common aspects as a means for change? You see, if you know what is more than likely to happen in any given circumstance, you would then be able to formulate a plan by which the outcome could be more favorable or changed forever. Could it be true that if we were able to educate citizens about such methods and behavior, they might avoid becoming victims altogether?

I was routinely asked to address homeowners' association meetings to talk about burglary prevention. I saw that the folks I had the honor of addressing were hungry for information. Often times my allotted presentation time was not nearly enough for me to answer all of the citizens questions and concerns. It was at this juncture that I realized a void. I saw the citizenry reacting and expressing a definitive need for more information. Citizens wanted and needed more in terms of understanding the crime of burglary. It wasn't just about a few burglary prevention tips; it was much more.

As an example, I would talk about the "typical burglary", "the truth about alarms" and "what to do if a burglar comes knocking at your door". All of these which are covered in this book. Most people had no idea of what I was talking about. The responses confirmed the lack of information and facts being provided to the citizens.

I began to research what police departments were doing to inform and educate citizens about burglary. I soon discovered that besides the generic statistical data and some basic home/business burglary prevention tips, there was nothing out there. In their defense, staffing and resources being limited and burglary being classified as a property crime, the priority is given to the "persons crimes" such as murder, rape and robbery.

I thus made the decision to put together a more comprehensive study of patterns of burglary and the behavior of burglars. My hope was that I could piece together all of these aspects and develop something that would not only help law enforcement in its efforts to combat the crime, but more importantly, to better assist and educate citizens with the tools needed to change the face of the crime. This book is written with that goal in mind.

CHAPTER TWO

*A*NATOMY OF A BURGLARY & BURGLAR

Anatomy of a Burglary

When talking with people about my experiences I found that many folks throughout the country have a different definition or description of burglary. When talking about burglary, I'm sure you have heard people say they were "robbed", short for robbery. Did you know? Robbery and burglary are two completely different crimes. In the State of Florida, the crime of Robbery is considered a person's crime or more specifically the taking of property by force or fear. Another common term for burglary is, "breaking and entering".

In any case, I thought it important to the nerds of the world to define the crime of burglary and include some statistical numbers to show its predominance. I'll try to be short and to the point. Total disclosure; my wife won't let me forget what a nerd I am.

Quick Note

It's important to note that the definitions and any classifications noted are my summarization of Florida State Statutes and/ or referenced from my work with the Miami-Dade Police Department in Miami, Florida. Statutes, definitions and/or classifications in other states or police departments could vary. It's important that you check with the law enforcement agency within your jurisdiction to answer any question you may have concerning these crimes or classifications.

So just to be clear, burglary is typically broken down into three categories; residential, commercial, and conveyance.

A residential burglary is one in which the burglar gains unlawful entry into your home, whether or not by force, and commits a crime therein. The crime therein generally refers to the theft of your personal property, or simply by the destruction of property, i.e.

breaking a window to gain entry also referred to as criminal mischief or vandalism.

A commercial burglary is one by which a business is targeted. The same elements of law apply concerning the unlawful entry to the business and commission of crime(s) therein.

A conveyance burglary would be that of a car, boat, RV, etc., where the same elements of law apply. You get the idea.

OK… So that wasn't so bad. Let's continue.

Did you know that according to the U.S. Department of Justice, Federal Bureau of Investigation statistical data, there are an average of 1,431,653 burglaries committed each year (2015-2018)? Of that, approximately 68.5% are residential burglaries. It's important to note that these figures fluctuate from year to year. From my personal knowledge of statistical data of burglaries and how each sub-category of the crime is reported, there can be varying totals. In the state of Florida, according to the Florida Department of Law Enforcement (FDLE), a burglary occurs on the average of every 5 minutes. Based on FDLE's reported burglaries from 2015 to 2018. 2019 to current date are still in process.

Anatomy of a Burglar

Often times people ask me to describe the "typical burglar". As a young boy growing up, I remember criminals being depicted as creepy looking individuals lurking the streets, usually dressed in dark colored clothing. I remember seeing cartoons that pictured individuals dawning masks and wearing long trench coats. Of course, Halloween would be the exception to any of the rules. This reminds of a time when I was a rooky officer working uniform patrol having my first experience with "appearances".

Looks are Deceiving

While driving on routine patrol a motorist driving a Cadillac made a left turn in front of me, causing me to brake suddenly to avoid a collision. I of course stopped the motorist who I will describe as a mature male dressed in a three-piece suit with the appearance of a businessman. As I approached him, he immediately apologized for turning in front of me and said he would certainly be more cautious in the future. As he acknowledged his error, I felt that I would merely conduct a routine record check of his driver license and let him on his way with a simple warning.

As I awaited the response on the record check, I heard the dispatcher sending several other units to me as back up. I was curious and advised the dispatcher that I was fine, thinking that perhaps I had missed a transmission checking on my well-being which was common practice for traffic stops. The dispatcher followed by informing me that the motorist was wanted for "Murder" and that I should exercise extreme caution as he might be armed.

As it turned out, the motorists was taken into custody without incident. I learned that the City of Miami P.D. along with the FBI and DEA had raided the man's home earlier in the day hoping to take him into custody. I contacted the lead detective on the case, and he thought I was joking about the apprehension as his colleagues had been teasing him about the failed raid. It didn't

take long to convince him that all turned out
well.

In the end, I learned that what appeared
to be a well-dressed businessman, was in fact
a fugitive on the run.

In my 29 years of experience and having arrested well over 1000 burglars, the typical burglar I arrested was predominantly male, ranging in age from 15-25, though I have dealt with burglars as young as 10 years of age and those into their 50's. Most came from low to medium socioeconomic backgrounds and struggled scholastically. A very high percentage of burglars I spoke with came from dysfunctional family environments and either experimented with or were actively using drugs and/or alcohol. In some cases, this dysfunction, or drug and alcohol abuse was the motivation for their chosen profession. Again, my description is purely based on my own experience and not meant to disparage any particular individual or group of individuals.

Interviews/Interrogations

With experience in Crime Scene Investigations and as a Hostage Negotiator with the Miami-Dade Special Response Team, I was able to marry my experience in forensic science and human behavior developing my own style of investigation and the interviewing/interrogation of burglars. Focus was placed on gaining rapport with the burglar and gaining insight to their methods and reasoning. Putting it all together was what helped me better learn and understand the anatomy of a burglar. I now share all of that with you.

Subject interviews were an integral part of my investigations and a good part of my success as an investigator. As you can imagine interviews were quite engaging. To give you an idea of what you might say was a "typical interview" let me paint the picture and outline how it would go.

Picture that most interviews were conducted in a room that was designed for that very purpose. Generally, a small sized room only large enough to accommodate a table with a couple of chairs. There are no pictures on the wall or music being pumped into the room. Not like anything you would see in Homes & Garden.

Typically, the first order of business is to get the paperwork out of the way. Most important was to present the subject with his or her Miranda Rights. I'm sure most of you are quite familiar with Miranda. Not to imply that you may have been arrested though we all have seen our fair share of reality TV cop shows. Did I mention I appeared on Miami Vice and Miami SWAT? But I regress.

Once the subject waived Miranda, meaning he or she agreed to speak with me without an attorney being present, the "interview/ interrogation" began. Again, with emphasis on human behavior I felt it first important to have what I like to call a, "let me get to know you" talk. There was no rush or pressure to immediately get a confession. It was much more important to first establish rapport with the subject to encourage better dialogue. This took some doing as you can imagine based on a number of factors though once rapport was established, the conversation just flowed. Of course, securing a confession was the number one objective though I also emphasized the need to discuss the issues of method and reasoning. I learned a lot by "listening" to what a burglar had to say. My grandmother would always say, "If your lips are moving, you're NOT listening".

A defense lawyer friend of mine I had known for a number of years once asked me how I was able to secure so many confessions. I remember smiling and saying, "It's Big Mac". He paused a second with a bit of a bewildered look on his face. I think he wondered for a moment who or what was I referring to. I smiled and said, "I feed them a Big Mac". You see, I had a McDonalds adjacent to my police station and I would always stop and get my arrestees what I called a "Happy Meal". Happy Meals went a long way for someone looking at eating bologna sandwiches and juice boxes in jail.

The Bubble Gum Burglar

Let me share with you a case that best depicted how my crime scene experience combined with interview method worked to convict a career criminal. The burglary was to a condominium in an upscale area of Miami. Entry had been made via the front door of the residence. It was a typical burglary in which the master bedroom had been ransacked and a quantity of property stolen.

The crime scene investigator processing the scene advised that he had not been able to find any latent fingerprints or other evidence that would have any prosecutorial value. This gave indication to the burglary having been committed by a career burglar.

As was routine, I conducted an area canvass of neighboring residences in an effort to gain further evidence and/or possible witnesses to the crime. As I knocked at the door of a neighboring condo and stood waiting for someone to answer I noticed a piece of bubble gum stuck in the peep hole. It happened to be a condo that faced the victim's residence. Are you starting to guess what happened?

I had crime scene impound the gum and process it for DNA. The result later revealed that the DNA matched that of a Career Criminal who happened to be now, weeks later, in custody in Broward County, Florida. Now let me explain the difference between a career burglar and Career

Criminal. What I refer to as a career burglar is one who routinely commits and is savvy to burglary. Whereas a Career Criminal is a title designated per Florida State Statute to an offender and carries enhanced penalties by law

This was great news though at the same time quite concerning. You see I knew that although the subject's gum was stuck in the peep hole of a neighboring condo, it didn't prove that he was the one who had committed the burglary. This compounded with the fact that I would be dealing with and having to secure a confession from a Career Criminal in jail. He would undoubtedly know that my case was weak given his criminal background.

I visited the subject at the Broward County Jail hoping for the best. Did I mention I wouldn't be able to bring him a Big Mac? Anyway, I sat down with him and decided my best approach would be a straightforward respectful conversation with empathy for his position. He acknowledged my tone of respect and then floored me with what followed. He explained that he had prayed to God the night before our meeting and had asked God to send someone with a message. He believed me to be that someone and what I had told him to be the message. Lastly, he agreed to give me a written confession which led to a plea deal of twelve years state prison.

If you're wondering what I had said to inspire him... I simply spoke honestly and appealed to him to settle his past acts in order to look forward to a new beginning.

I'm reminded of one other unique interview of a subject that had a lot to do with rapport and just having a simple conversation. The interview had turned to more of a conversation about his life and troubles with family. After having talked for quite a while he asked, "Aren't you going to ask me about the burglary?" It was crazy. He was actually asking me to take his confession.

The Why?

The why burglars commit burglaries always seemed to come up in conversations with victims. I can tell you that the very common perception was that all burglars were drug addicts and were in desperate need of money for their next fix. Of course, some did choose to commit burglaries in order to finance their drug habit, though the majority said it was purely for financial gain.

Those burglars who struggled with drug addiction spoke of searching victim's homes not only for the cash, jewelry and such, though also rummaged through medicine cabinets for drugs. They bragged about finding a plethora of drugs in many of the homes they burglarized. Something to think about.

Some burglars expressed a feeling of exhilaration or high, as a reason for their actions. The same reason for why they graduated to occupied burglaries commonly committed at night or in the early morning hours and referred to as "Cat Burglaries". I will discuss this in more detail later

Some burglars said it was simply their job, same as anyone's chosen profession. When interviewing one burglar, he bragged about committing burglaries Monday thru Friday like a 9 to 5 and taking the weekends off. He was also proud to say that he attended church on Sundays.

The most common reason or word and that which I found to be most informative was that it was simply, easy.

Think of that… easy. Merriam-Webster's dictionary defines easy as, "causing or involving little difficulty or discomfort. Within easy reach. Requiring or indicating little effort, thought, or reflection".

As I pressed burglars for their interpretation of easy; they spoke of how easy it was to gain entry to one's home, easy to take their property/money and an easy way to get what they wanted. They bragged about how easy people made it for them to do what they do, even when people had alarms and all forms of security, or so they thought.

With this definition and understanding of burglary and those who commit the crime, we will now get into the details of how it all affects you. Not only a crime of property loss, but as a crime that violates your very person. A crime that has a profound effect on you, your family and even your neighbors.

CHAPTER THREE

*Y*OUR HOME, BUSINESS AND VEHICLE

As previously noted, the focus of this book will be on residential burglary. Residential burglary accounts for the majority of burglaries committed among classes of burglary and is, in my opinion, the most profound as it's the one that usually creates the feeling of a personal crime/attack. Casting the deeper feeling of violation. In this chapter, I will provide you with what I have found to be the most common or typical in a residential burglary including other scenarios.

A "Typical" Residential Burglary

Over the course of my career I have seen thousands of burglaries. Some which were quite unique in nature. For now, let's focus on what I consider to be "a typical residential burglary" as to the method of operation (M.O.) that burglars tend to follow.

First, did you know that most residential burglaries occur during daylight hours when families are generally not present at home due to work or school. Versus nighttime "Cat Burglaries". These are rare and generally committed by burglars who are "escalating" their actions in order to obtain more of a "thrill". I will address this and other burglary scenarios in more detail later.

Burglars select their targets by driving, biking or even jogging through a neighborhood. Most said driving was their preferred mode of transportation though some said it was better to ride around on a bike or jog. I understood their reasoning as people are more likely to notice an "unknown" car to the neighborhood. I can't tell you how many times a surveillance that I was on was "burned" due to neighbors whom became suspicious of my "unmarked" police car. I remember one time someone asking me if I was the "real police". Thinking of it, at the time I was somewhat bewildered by the question. Time for another story.

This was truly a concern for some citizens of Miami back in the day of Home-Invasions. A Home-Invasion Robbery, not a burglary, is one in which the subject(s) enter your home with intent to commit a robbery and are usually armed. The big little detail to the robbery was that the subjects would be dressed as police as a means of entering the residence. Picture several men dawning badges, raid jackets and let's not forget the guns yelling police as they pushed their way into your home.

The same sort of scheme was also being used to stop motorists on the road. Using red/ blue flashing lights the subjects would pull over unsuspecting motorist and then rather than having to present your driver's license and registration, you were being forced to give up your wallet.

Burglars survey a number of factors, mainly the nature of the neighborhood in which you reside, i.e. do the homes appear as if the owners would have property of value. Burglars also tend to prefer a neighborhood where there is little chance of their presence alerting anyone. Burglars gravitate towards homes that offer an "inviting" presence, no one at home, no vehicles in the driveway, landscaping which covers/conceals entry/exit points, or packages left at the door by delivery services such as UPS or Amazon. Not to mention the obvious, such as a number of newspapers left outside, or a mailbox stuffed to capacity.

In a typical burglary, two to three subjects typically commit burglaries working in concert with each other. Each having his or her designated task whether it is acting as a look out, one who makes entry to the home or enters and removes property

Burglars generally don't want to be confronted by anyone within the home, not to mention it usually enhances the criminal penalties when the home is occupied. Burglars will typically take steps to assure the home is vacant and typically be bold enough to knock at your door or ring the doorbell to see if anyone answers.

This is a critical juncture in the burglary as it enfolds you or your loved ones, particularly children who may be home alone. I will be covering this issue in more detail in chapter four; Education & Having a Plan.

Once the burglars have determined no one is home, they will proceed to make entry by whatever means necessary. Most burglars have their own preferred method of entering the home whether it be boldly kicking in the front door or breaking and/or prying a window or sliding glass door. Some are lock picks. Generally, they prefer to pick a point of entry that is hidden from line of sight; a location whereby someone either walking or driving by would not see them. They usually scout a point of entry on the side or rear of your home where they feel even a neighbor would not readily be able to see them

As this is happening, a lookout will usually keep watch on the front of the home from a comfortable distance down the road in order to alert his/her partners of anyone approaching the residence, such as your children returning home from school, you from work, a postal/ special delivery, friend or neighbor and of course the POLICE.

Once inside your home, the subject(s) will focus on identifying and ransacking the master bedroom. As they know this is the place where most of us keep our valuables, such as jewelry, cash and weapons. A burglar will do this with precision and speed knowing that the police may very well be on the way to apprehend them. Most all the burglars I interviewed said they could commit a burglary in five to ten minutes. Many bragged about taking less time. Time is what I call the big little detail of burglaries.

> *Keeping in mind what we have learned about the typical burglar, we are usually dealing with a teenager or young adult, one who has claimed to be both fast and efficient in the execution of the crime and one who is able to commit the crime in about five minutes or less. Here's the kicker; not even the best of alarm systems can manipulate time. So, although alarm systems may act as a deterrent to some, we need to be aware that it is not the holy grail of burglary prevention. Every burglar that I interviewed was very aware of time. Most felt that they could beat the clock entering and exiting long before the police arrived.*

Most burglars travel light, placing their bounty (your valuables) in either a backpack that they brought with them or perhaps one of your own pillowcases. That's not to say they'll pass up on taking a widescreen tv, computers, or gaming systems. This will all depend on the liking or comfort level of the burglar.

After taking whatever has caught their eye, they will call for the "look out" to pick them up.

Within just a few minutes time, the burglars will have impacted your life, and that of your family, for years to come. Not by mere financial loss or damage to your home, but by the feeling of having been personally violated. It is for this very reason that I decided to do everything in my power to inform, educate and prepare you in hopes that together we can change the face of this property crime to a very personal one.

Other Residential Burglary Scenarios

Let's now touch on some of the other burglary scenarios that occur from time to time.

Cat Burglaries

As previously noted, nighttime or Cat Burglaries, are committed during the late-night hours while victims are sound asleep in their beds. In most cases, a single individual commits a cat burglary. One seeking an exhilarating experience. In other words, the property crime committed therein is only secondary to the thrill being sought by the intruder. The burglar is entering your home knowing that he or she is doing so with the expectation of walking throughout your home while you and perhaps other family are present.

In the course of interviewing many of these subjects, they made it clear to me that they had become bored with committing daytime burglaries. Some subjects would even say that the daytime burglaries they committed became just too easy and common. Many would describe how exhilarating it was to be standing in a victim's bedroom watching, as people were asleep in their bed. The subjects described a feeling of euphoria as they could feel their heart racing.

Some subjects went as far as to make physical contact with the victim as they slept and in some rare cases, the subjects would go as far as to masturbate as they stood over their victims. There could never be a clearer example of how the subject demeans a victim and in turn causes the victim to feel demeaned: a personal crime indeed.

Generally, victims whom had awoken to the sight of a stranger standing in their bedroom spoke of yelling out in fear, anger, or both; the result of which caused the burglar to quickly flee the residence. Of course, there were those whom had awoken in the morning to the realization that they had been burglarized. Usually the victims were not physically harmed, but in any case, the burglar had certainly left a mark on the victims internally.

This type of burglary is of special concern, as you can imagine.

The individuals committing this type of burglary are escalating their actions by committing a crime that now threatens physical harm to victims. Therefore, cat burglaries are given priority and a number of additional resources are provided to assist in the identification and apprehension of the subject(s) responsible.

Distraction Burglary

In distraction burglaries the burglar will walk up to the front door of the residence and make contact with the victim. Once the victim comes to the door, the burglar explains that he/she has been contracted by the neighboring property to trim the trees and/or clear foliage. The burglar then kindly asks if he/she could access the victim's back yard in an effort to make sure that the victim's property will be protected from any peripheral issues or damages. Most victims are eager to accept this proposal, as, on its face value, it is for the protection of their own property. Most victims see it even as very thoughtful.

Once the victim agrees, the burglar will ask the victim to accompany him/her to the backyard for the safety inspection. What the victim is unaware of is that as the burglar is talking a good game and keeping the victim occupied in the backyard, the burglar's accomplice will be making entry to the front of the residence, usually via a now unlocked front door, and steal the victim's property. Once the burglar has stolen the victim's valuables, he/she will signal the other via cell phone or even a blow of the horn from their vehicle, that it's time to leave. Once gone, the victim usually just goes about his/her business and might not notice their missing property for some time.

Some other scenarios involved telling the victim there was a rodent infestation in the neighborhood or construction soon to begin. Remember the key to this type of burglary is to gain entry to your home by providing some type of story that would seem credible to any reasonable person. Once inside, the burglar has what he/she wants; access to your valuables.

The elderly are more prone to distraction burglaries. Burglars prey upon the elderly as they believe them to be more gullible and less capable of identifying them or pursuing a prosecution. Not to mention, elders usually have acquired quite a bit of fine jewelry over their lifetime that they expect to pass down to their love ones.

Cyclical/Seasonal Burglaries

One other burglary scenario I would like to cover is something I refer to as *cyclical/seasonal burglaries*. These are burglaries which occur as result of some type of cyclical event or season of the year. The obvious would be holidays such as Christmas. Burglars love Christmas shopping just as much as anyone. The only problem is that they shop at your home or business, not the mall. I know most of us love to decorate for Christmas and place all of the presents under the tree. Often your tree is placed in front of a window of your home within view of all passing by. The tree and presents on display mirroring a store window showcase.

Another cyclical/seasonal event is when the circus or fair is in town. Attracting cash carrying attendees and criminals ready to take advantage. In this scenario vehicle burglaries and/or theft is of concern. To combat this, my unit would conduct enhanced enforcement initiatives to patrol the parking lots and grounds of these events. We arrested a number of vehicle burglars and auto thieves in the course of the operation.

You get the idea; cyclical/seasonal burglaries could be associated with any event that brings with it, opportunity for burglars. The lesson here is to be aware of these types of situations and be cautious.

Fumigation (Tenting) Burglaries

Finally, I would like to cover a scenario that although rare, nevertheless occurred with enough frequency that I felt I should include it. The scenario is fumigation (tenting) burglaries. For example, when a home is tented for let's say termites, there are burglars that will cut through the tenting and enter your home. Crazy, right? So, should you ever have your home tented, it might be a good idea to share this information with your neighbors and have them keep an eye on your home.

Outside the realm of a typical burglary and the other scenarios I have talked about, I wanted to close this segment by sharing with you the story of a burglar and the burglaries that he committed which I found to be unique in nature. The case set itself apart from anything else I had ever come upon in my twenty-nine-year career. The burglar's method of operation was to commit a burglary as if it had never happened.

The burglar's methods were just a part of the unusual nature of the crimes he committed. What was even more bizarre was the connection he had to his family, both living and deceased. I call the story A Message from Beyond. I will leave it up to you to draw whatever conclusions you may or may not have about the man or beyond.

A Message from Beyond

The story is about a family man, who had lost his job and was desperate to make some money in order to feed his wife and newborn baby girl. The subject had committed in excess of forty residential burglaries utilizing quite a unique method of operation (M.O.)

Every day he would leave his home in the morning, give a loving kiss to his wife and little girl, saying he was going off to work. He would drive to a particular neighborhood that he had come to feel comfortable in and park his vehicle alongside the road. He would then venture out on foot in search of a home to burglarize. His goal was to find a residence that had an unlocked or open door/window. He would enter the residence via this unlocked/open point of entry and then very neatly search the victim's master bedroom furnishings and closet in search of cash and jewelry. His neatness itself was key, as I will explain.

He was very selective in taking only a very few precious jewels in hope of getting a greater return at a local pawn shop. This was key to his M.O. Once he gathered some jewelry and perhaps cash, he then exited the residence the same way he had entered.

Here comes the uniqueness of the burglary. Most of the victims would return home and not even notice that a burglary had been committed. The home appeared just as they had left it. It wasn't until the victim went to retrieve a particular piece of jewelry or their cash that was kept in the back of their nightstand drawer, did he/she realize it had been stolen. Remember the common burglar ransacks the room. So, in essence some of these neat or tidy burglaries were reported days after having been committed as a result of this guy's tidiness.

In the end, some good old-fashioned police work and cooperating neighborhood watch people led to the subject's vehicle description and license plate number.

Once arrested, his first arrest, the subject broke down crying and had quite a story to tell. You see the subject's wife's father had recently died and was buried in a cemetery that bordered the neighborhood where the subject had been committing the burglaries. In the course of his interrogation, the subject told my fellow detective and me that just days before, his wife had woken him up in the middle of the night in a frantic state having had a dream that had brought her to tears. His wife told him that her father had come to her in a dream to tell her that her husband was doing very bad things and that their lives were about to be devastated. Certainly, turned out to be true.

Businesses

I had the honor of working with many business owners over the years and know that each and every one was a hard-working individual and well invested in their business. Of course, my meeting with these owners usually came as result of their business having been burglarized. I found that many owners and/or managers were unaware of many aspects of commercial burglary. Time and time again I would investigate cases that I felt could have been avoided if only there had been a greater awareness and/or preventative measures taken. That said, I will cover all of the aspects of this crime that I feel, given my experience, are worthy of discussion.

A business burglary, commonly referred to as a commercial burglary by police departments, is a crime that is more correctly designated as a property crime as we are dealing with a place of business and not your "personal" residence. Although I must say that I have handled cases whereby the owner or an employee of the business did in fact reside there as well. Also, residential/business construction sites fall into this category. I will cover each area respectively.

The burglars usual focus here is to target either money left in a cash register or safe, or products in inventory. Most commercial burglaries occur during late-night hours when no employees or customers, are present. Many commercial burglars have told me that they preferred committing commercial burglary to residential burglary as they felt more confident working in an environment likely to be absent of people and under the cover of darkness (night).

There are a number of ways commercial burglars make entry to a business. More common would be to break a window or door glass or pry a door open. Others make entry by breaking through a wall of a neighboring business with lesser security measures. When your business sides with other businesses, as in a strip mall, the adjoining walls are generally built of drywall. A burglar can simply kick the drywall out and bingo, he/she has made entry to your business. When breaking through glass or a wall is not your thing, there is always the roof. That's right, the roof. Many burglars will access the roof of a business to find a point of entry, such as an air conditioning duct or a skylight.

Finally, I have to mention the old drive through the front doors with a stolen vehicle method of entry. This was popular until businesses started to install reinforced concrete pillars in front of the doors.

A different kind of Drive Thru

This brings to mind a couple of cases. In one, a department store was the target. The subjects drove a vehicle through the entrance and then what appeared to be (per video surveillance footage) at least six subjects, running into the store and grabbing as much clothing from the display racks as each could hold. You may notice that some department stores now tend to hang clothing on racks located close to entry/exit doors with the hangers staggered. Making it difficult for someone to grab an abundance of clothing at one time.

In another case, after driving the vehicle through the door of a sporting goods store, several subjects ran into the store and stole a

As you can see, burglars can be quite intent on gaining entry to a business they have targeted. As I investigated each case and its related method of entry it was clear that the burglar had assessed the security of each location and with that surmised the best way to break in. The common term being, casing the business.

After having gained entry to the business, the burglar(s) will proceed to target that in which they have interest. Anything from cash to product or both. What determined this was in large part related to what kind of business was burglarized. For example, restaurants were routinely burglarized in an effort to acquire cash that was kept in a cash drawer, register or a safe. Electronics stores were targeted mostly for their inventory of the latest hot items such as computers, game stations, cell phones and the like.

Now that I have covered some of the basics and commonalities of commercial burglary, I want to take you through some steps that you may want to consider taking to better secure your business. To do this I want you to start with casing your business. That's right, if a burglar can do it, why can't you. This is the first step in securing your business. You have to take an objective view of your business and decide if you were going to "break in" to your establishment, how would you do it? Given the methods of entry I have outlined, what do you think? This will entail surveying the property and taking each possible method of entry and making the appropriate changes to deter the burglary.

Take the most common method of breaking a door/window glass. You may want to change the glass to impact resistant glass, sometimes referred to as hurricane windows. This type of glass is made to withstand winds of up to 200 mph and of course withstand strikes from flying debris. The window will sustain damage though it will hold its integrity as a barrier.

There are other options depending on your budget and/or restrictions should you be leasing the space for your business. For example, I have seen businesses install shutters that shield the store front from not only intrusion, but also inclement weather such as hurricanes.

As you continue to survey your business, consider reviewing the "Burglary Awareness & Prevention" chapter of this book. There

I cover many other topics such as alarm systems, surveillance video, safes, structural barriers and a concept called "Crime Prevention Through Environmental Design". It will offer you a guide as to what you may consider right for your business.

Next, I want to highlight areas that I consider important and specific to commercial burglary such as doors, locks, roof access and lighting.

Unlike the doors in your home, businesses obviously deal with a number of more commercial type doors which can be constructed of glass or steel. I covered glass breaks to doors so let's talk about a door pry. Simply put, burglars tend to use a pry bar which they insert between the door and frame and pry the two apart in order to defeat the lock. I know some businesses utilize some type of "pry guard" that is basically a steel plate covering the vulnerable area of the door. This may be something to consider though nothing is fool proof. As I would tell citizens, every little bit helps. A good burglary prevention plan has many "layers" of security employed.

Another type of door pry is what would be referred to as "peeling the door". This is a method by which the burglar literally peels the door open. This is generally accomplished by using a tow hook.

Riding in Style

I was assigned to a multi-agency investigation of a commercial burglary ring that specialized in this type of entry to commit a number of burglaries to major electronics stores throughout the tri-county area of South Florida. The subjects rented high end cars such as BMW's and Lexus', as their mode of transportation. At least they had style. The method here was to back a vehicle to the rear delivery entrance door of the business and connect a tow hook from the vehicle to the bottom corner of the door. They would then pull the vehicle forward and "peel" the corner of the door outward. This created a space large enough to gain access. Once inside, the subjects would waste no time in targeting what they came for.

I should mention that although the business had surveillance video, the subjects had taken measures to conceal their identity. In the end, as in most cases, we ultimately identified and arrested the individuals involved despite their efforts to conceal their identity.

Frat Boys

In another case, I dealt with a couple of burglars whom had committed multiple commercial burglaries to electronics stores utilizing a number of door pry methods. This was a unique case as the subjects were well educated individuals who had attended a private preparatory school together and had decided to commit burglaries for a living. In preparation for their desire to be a successful crime duo, they studied locksmith books and engineering related to door structures. They also studied crime scene investigation to develop methods by which to avoid identification by forensic science. I had never seen so much effort invested in the pursuit of a commercial burglary. So, you must be wondering, how did they get caught? You see, as I had mentioned earlier, burglars usually "case" the business prior to the actual

So, what does all of this mean to you? Given your budget and whether you own or lease, you have a number of options. When dealing with entry/exit points an important consideration would be that of laws in your jurisdiction relating to access/egress for employees/patrons of the business. This is especially of concern for fire safety measures. After a review of these issues you will be better equipped to formulate a plan to reinforce and/or install additional physical barriers.

Next, let's discuss door locks. There are a number of commercial grade door locks to pick from. The only thing I would highlight here is that if at all possible, you pick a lock (no pun intended) that offers some type of additional security as opposed to the common lock.

Another thing to consider related to locks would be key control. The key to your business should be protected at all cost. You can spend thousands of dollars installing all kinds of security measures though should you not maintain proper key control, it could be all for nothing. One step in key control would be to have a lock/key system that provides keys which are not readily copied without proper identification. Again, not fool proof, but one more layer of protection. Finally, be careful who you trust with the keys to your business. I investigated many cases involving disgruntled employees who betrayed the trust given to them by an owner and/or manager of a business. Change or re-key the locks of your business each time an employee with key access has been terminated or if a key is lost. Or perhaps look into "keyless" locks which allow you to change the lock codes.

Now, let's talk about roof access. First, please be careful when trying to access the roof of your business. I would suggest taking any and all safety measures available. Once you access the roof, you would want to inspect any access points such as air conditioning units and skylights. I would suggest you have a licensed and insured contractor conduct this survey with you, as prevention barriers would entail some type of construction tying into the roof structure itself.

Finally, I would like to talk about lighting. Remember, most burglars that commit commercial burglaries have told me they do so due to the advantage of working under the cover of darkness (night). Of course, to do this you need to "case" your business at night. You want to make sure any existing lighting is sufficient in fully illuminating all entry/exit points of the business and even the roof area if at all possible. Also, leave the interior lights of your business on at night. In order to conserve energy costs, consider "motion activated" and/or LED lighting for the business. You may also want to consider leaving only a number of interior lights on that offer some illumination of the business. I have seen businesses that have the ability to turn on/off every other light throughout the store. The midnight shift patrol officer will be very grateful as well.

Quick Note

Have you ever entered a room and turned on the light to find roaches scatter? In my business, I visited places that were very displeasing to say it politely. Anyway, I couldn't help relating this to burglars trying to move around in darkness. They avoid the light!

Construction Sites

Finally, let's talk about construction sites such as newly constructed residential subdivisions. Construction sites are classified as commercial burglary and are a big business for commercial burglar rings. Here burglars target sites where they can find new equipment such as air conditioning units and home appliances. The majority of these burglaries are committed during the late-night hours and favor the weekend, though I have investigated a few committed during the daylight hours when construction workers were not present.

It became quite clear to us in the Department that we were getting a lot of new construction cases involving the theft of either appliances and/or air conditioning units. Of course, as with all newly identified crime trends we were directed to develop a strategy to combat this issue. Contractors began to delay installation of the new appliances until just prior to a home being inspected for a certificate of occupancy (CO). This minimized exposure to burglary/theft.

Double Dating

In one of my master cases, a master case being one whereby multiple burglaries (cases) are ultimately found to be committed by the same individual(s) over a period of time, multiple homes were getting hit and appliances were the target. After reviewing the facts of these cases, it was determined that the subject(s) had to have intimate knowledge of the installation dates/times of the appliances. Furthermore, common sense would dictate that the subject vehicle being used to execute these burglaries would have to be of a size to accommodate the load. Also, all of the homes being targeted were in a specific area of Miami-Dade County enabling us to better focus resources such as uniform patrol units working within that zone.

Given the excellent work of our uniform officers in the specific area of concern, we soon identified a vehicle that matched in several aspects related to the burglaries. The owner/operator of the vehicle (a van) was identified as a construction worker who had been employed in all of the specific areas and/or job sites where the burglaries were occurring.

I secured a court order to place a GPS tracker on the van in question. It soon became apparent that the location of the van matched the location of burglaries that followed. Also, at one of the locations a crowbar used to gain access to the residence was left behind. The crowbar was submitted to the lab for latent and DNA processing. This proved to be helpful in the prosecution of the individual.

Ultimately a surveillance of the subject resulted in his arrest and that of his accomplices who happened to be a co-worker and their respective girlfriends. That's right, the girlfriends were acting hand in hand to commit the burglaries. Love knows no bounds. In the end, one of the girls decided her love for her boyfriend was not as strong as her desire to avoid a prison term. Accepting a plea deal (prosecutorial agreement), the girlfriend testified as a witness for the State resulting in convictions of her co-defendants.

Conveyance Burglary

I would be remiss not to cover conveyance burglaries. Again, conveyance meaning motor vehicle, boat, trailer, plane, etc. My emphasis will be on motor vehicle, (car) burglaries.

As you can imagine, car burglaries occur mostly in the night hours though a good number do occur during daytime hours as well, generally in business or shopping mall parking lots.

Car Hopping

Let's first talk about nighttime car burglaries. The latest craze for car burglaries is what juveniles and young adults call "car hopping". This is where a group of teens/young adults work as a group to cover a specific neighborhood in search of cars with unlocked doors. They typically park their vehicle in the area of the targeted neighborhood and set out on foot going from home to home, pulling on car door handles. Once they find an unlocked car, they ransack the interior in search of property. As you can imagine, a great number of burglaries can be committed in short time in this scenario because the burglars are able to canvass several blocks of area in a very short time.

The defense against this type of car burglary is simply to lock your car doors. I have tirelessly tried to convey this message to citizens and victims of burglary. The general excuse is that they believe if they were to lock their car doors, a burglar would break their window to get into the car. And when mentioning the broken window, people often say they would have to bear the cost of a repair in addition to the loss of their property.

The fact of the matter is that if you choose to keep your car doors unlocked, you should not store any valuables in your car. Victims have reported everything from loose change, sunglasses, to computers and yes firearms taken in a car burglary. The last thing we need is another firearm in the hands of criminals. Please be responsible. It's your choice. As they say, "an ounce of prevention is worth a pound of cure."

A Burglar's Shopping Spree

Finally, I want to mention a scenario of car burglary that is common to shopping mall parking lots and notably electronics stores, especially during the holiday season. Typically, car burglars will walk through the rows of vehicles in search of an opportunity. Many car burglars have told me that they are just glancing into cars as they walk through the parking lot. Once they find a car with some kind of property of interest, like a purse or shopping bag, they will try the door handle. If the car is locked, some will proceed to break into the car by a variety of means.

Burglars will also just sit and watch a parking lot in hopes of seeing you exit with a number of shopping bags that you are carrying out to your car. Better yet, if you have just purchased that great new computer or television, it will become what they were really wishing and waiting for. The burglar watches to see if you are going to leave the car and return to shopping for more goodies or are you going to drive to the next store or restaurant before returning home. That's right, burglars are known to surveil you and follow you in hopes of being able to take your purchases. Should you leave your vehicle unattended at that time or at any subsequent stop you make, the burglar will then leap into action and break into your car.

A Group Effort

This brings to mind a story about groups of individuals, predominantly from South America, that would travel to Miami every holiday season with the purpose of committing a rash of vehicle burglaries

These individuals worked in concert with each other to surveil and subsequently burglarize victims. Imagine that just as law enforcement conducts surveillance of suspects, these individuals were acting in the

The moral to the story is to be aware of your surroundings. As you exit a store and walk to your car, take note of anything that sparks your interest. It could be someone following you or sitting around with no purpose. You should not leave your purchases, especially big-ticket items such as electronics, unattended in your car. Placing your valuables and/or purchases in the trunk of your car is an added bit of security and deterrent to burglars.

In closing this chapter, I hope that by highlighting what I would consider the most likely scenarios of residential, business and car burglary that you will avoid becoming a victim. Again, this is all about awareness. Awareness leads to prevention.

CHAPTER FOUR

BURGLARY AWARENESS & PREVENTION

Burglary awareness and prevention is one of the most talked about aspects of burglary because every home or business owner deals with it on some level or another. It's something that you are confronted with on a daily basis whether you realize it or not. You are thinking about prevention in everything from securing your personal items to locking your doors or watching the myriad of television commercials that want you to believe their product is the best in keeping you and your family safe. To become aware is to be better equipped to prevent. How can you prevent anything from occurring without first being aware of what you are dealing with?

There are a multitude of topics to consider when discussing burglary awareness and prevention. I will cover those topics which I have found to be the most fundamental and important to consider when contemplating what burglary prevention methods are best for you. These include alarm systems, video, storing your valuables, safes, pets, crime prevention through environmental design (CPTED), structural barriers, Crime Watch groups and your neighbors. I refer to all of these as layers of security. It is my hope to have you consider security overall as being layered. Also, ideally you should not rely on any one layer in and of itself. So, as I cover each topic remember it is just another layer of security.

It's also very important for me to address the issue of cost as it relates to any layer of security suggested. The cost of securing your home or business can be overwhelming to say the least. That is not to say that one would not be able to incorporate a good system at low cost. Some security measures in and of themselves come at little or no cost at all, perhaps being the most sensible to enact for starters. Again, I will reiterate that no matter what systems/layers you decide to incorporate, do so with the understanding that success comes with not being dependent on any one system/layer alone.

Within this chapter I will also teach you some basic fundamentals in educating your love ones and having a plan in place in the event that burglars present themselves at your doorstep with intent to enter your home. As I have previously mentioned, many children are told not to answer a knock at the door when home alone.

This being perhaps the worst course of action when considering the fact that burglars routinely knock at the door prior to making entry to the home.

Aside from all of these methods, what is most important to burglary awareness and prevention is to believe in your own sense of awareness. We all have it in us to be aware and sense when something is either right or wrong. On countless occasions throughout my career and personal life, I have heard people talking about how they had a feeling or that they knew something wasn't right. Some refer to it as a gut feeling, hunch, women's intuition, psychic ability and yes even Spidey senses. You pick the phrase. In all, your sense of awareness was peaked.

Given this sense of awareness, I like to coin the phrase, You Know It in Your Knower. This is what I believe to be the best description of what many victims and witnesses would convey in regard to a feeling they had. And so, as you read through this book and become aware of how the information contained herein relates to you, remember above all you know it in your knower. Believe in yourself and boldly take action.

Alarm Systems

Some of the most popular questions victims would ask me were about alarm systems for the home or business. In order for me to properly cover this subject, I think it best to first take you through the steps of what occurs when an alarm is activated. Keep in mind that what I am going to outline for you is based on what I would refer to as the most common system(s) I encountered throughout my career, as well is the police response outlined. Systems and Police Department responses will vary across the nation. I encourage you to verify what is common practice in your area

Once an intruder has entered your home via a door or window, most alarm systems will delay notifying the police of a possible intrusion. The most common delay is 45 seconds. This is done to give you, or anyone you have authorized to enter, enough time to get to the alarm panel and enter a secret squirrel code, thus cancelling further action or the call for police. If the code is not entered in time, the alarm will activate. The monitoring call center will now place a telephone call to the residence and/or your cellular phone, in order of your pre-selected order of contact. If unable to make contact or if someone does answer the phone and doesn't give the correct secret squirrel code word, the call center will proceed to notify the police.

You may be wondering why the call center doesn't just immediately call the police. This call is made to verify whether you, your children or a guest accidently tripped the alarm by entering the wrong secret squirrel code. Believe me, it happens. Simply put, a lot of people have trouble with inputting a code or have out of town visitors or house sitters that forget your instructions. Not to mention, most police agencies responding to alarms will charge you for a false activation. This could become very expensive.

Now getting back to the order of what happens. The call center contacts the police to alert of the possible intrusion usually via some dedicated land or cellular line established for this very purpose. You may want to inquire as to how your alarm company or call center makes the notification. In Miami-Dade, the call is made to the county communications complaint desk and the information is taken by a complaint officer and then forwarded to the police dispatcher. The dispatcher in turn checks for availability of road patrol units and dispatches the call accordingly, presumably one that is in close proximity to the location. This, of course, is in a perfect world. Need I say more.

The officer responds as routine (no lights and sirens) and follows proper protocols to check on the residence or business. Again, this would pertain to a routine alarm call. I make this point because many television Cop shows, or movies show police responding to alarms at high speed with lights and sirens blazing. This gives many the impression of what common practice in the real world would be, which is not the case or protocol.

What is most important about this explanation of alarm systems and the response to the same is TIME. Time is of the essence, right? So again, let's go through the steps:

- Alarm activation
- 45 second delay
- Alarm Company/Call Center attempts to contact you
- Alarm Company/Call Center contacts the police Complaint Desk if attempt fails
- Complaint Desk takes the call and pertinent information
- Complaint Officer forwards alarm call to the police dispatcher
- Call is dispatched to appropriate Patrol Officer
- Officer responds accordingly

Once you start to add up the seconds and minutes through each step you can see, just as a burglar knows, it may indeed take some time for the police to arrive on scene.

At this point I should make it clear that there are various types of alarm designations. The alarm could be classified as audible. Meaning the alarm is audibly ringing or buzzing at the location alerting not only the burglars, but your neighbors as well. You know, like the ones you have heard in your neighborhood more commonly coming from a car. The ones everyone tends to ignore or is pissed-off about because it is interrupting their favorite TV show or the game.

Another type of alarm designation is a silent alarm. This of course is self-explanatory and as the word implies, there is no audible sounding of the alarm.

Another designation is a panic alarm. This refers to an alarm most often set off by the homeowner who is at home and suffering a burglary in progress. This may also be accompanied by a telephone call from the homeowner, in which case, the alarm would be reclassified as a verified burglary in progress and protocol would allow for an emergency response (lights and siren). This would be somewhat similar to a hold-up alarm. A designation more often assigned when a bank teller or business cashier activates an alarm by depressing or activating a switch.

Along with any of these designations a secondary designation may follow such as motion detection or glass break. These are again self-explanatory. Motion detectors within the residence or business have detected motion, supposedly by that of an intruder. The breaking of a window, equipped with sensors, would also activate the system.

I have responded to many motion detection alarms that turn out to be a pet that has gotten out of its crate. Or in the case of a business, the air conditioner register pointed towards some sort of signage has caused the system to interpret the waving sign as an intruder.

Now that you have a basic understanding of alarms and the response that follows an activation, I think it's important to discuss some of the types of alarms and features that are offered. I could probably write another book on the different systems and features though I will try to limit the discussion to what would be basic need.

Currently alarms are basically either wireless or hardwired. You have undoubtedly seen the plethora of Smart Alarm systems currently available that are advertised, allowing you to watch an intruder in real time via your cell phone and even allow you to talk to/warn the intruder that the police have been called and are on the way. Oh, and let's not forget the ones that mimic a dog barking. The wireless systems seem to be dominating the industry as not only do they serve as alarms for burglary, they also wirelessly connect to many other systems within your home such as interior/exterior lighting, thermostat control and toilet flush. Just kidding, they can't flush your toilet…yet.

Whether wireless or hardwired the primary function of systems is to first have a deterrent value, that is to deter burglars from entering your home or business and second to alert you (alarm) as to the presence of a possible or real threat.

In order to accomplish these goals, the first line of defense is the posting of signs in your yard or adjacent to doors/windows, as well the TV commercials themselves that illustrate the systems performance and capability. It's the scarecrow effect that's being sought. Secondly, to alert you as to possible or real threats either system relies on a series of sensors whether physical or motion activated.

What follows is what I refer to as the basic set up. Again, keep in mind that both wireless and hardwired systems serve well. The only consideration would be price point.

Quick Note

Keep in mind as you inquire about alarm systems and watch the amusing commercials, burglars are inquiring and watching the same commercials. Just food for thought.

The more common and basic set up of an alarm would include contact points on all of your doors and windows. Hard wired systems would also include an alarm panel from which you would activate/ deactivate or monitor your system and a central alarm box which maintains all of the connections (wiring) for your system which is usually installed in your master bedroom closet. I will address this further in a minute. Another basic I feel to be very important is an independent signal transmitter with its own independent battery back-up. This is because many alarms utilize the telephone or computer lines in your home/business to alert the call center which can be defeated.

Most burglars expressed familiarity with how to defeat the alarm by cutting or disconnecting the telephone/cable lines on the exterior of a residence similar to the plastic pin plug used inside your home. In the event that the telephone line and/or electricity has been interrupted the independent system will still transmit the alarm activation.

To be clear, throughout this book I will avoid revealing certain techniques that burglars use to defeat security measures such as alarms, video, locks, etc. I don't want to give any burglars further ideas that they haven't already come up with. The methods discussed are those which 99.9% of the burglars I have interviewed over the years already know and utilize. Furthermore, it is imperative that you have a certain degree of knowledge concerning a burglar's methods in order for you to be better prepared.

So now that I have covered the basics you can understand that we have created a system that will alert of an intruder who enters your home/business by opening a door or window, thus breaking the "contact" that's in place. But what if the burglar enters the door or window without opening it? Translation; the burglar breaks through the door panel/glass or window pane. Now you might want to consider adding the glass break sensors that we spoke about. As well, you might want to consider interior motion sensors depending on your particular setting i.e., pets or those fancy automatic vacuum cleaners that run around the home while you are at work or play. Although I must say that most smart systems can now adapt to pet movement.

All in all, the options for alarm design are endless as is the price point. Keep in mind that you may also be dealing with additional costs such as monitoring services or government fees for registering your alarm. Not to mention fines imposed for false alarm responses.

I have to say that many burglars boast that alarms are not the end all deterrent. Some burglars claim they like entering homes with alarms. Translation; homeowners with alarms have a false sense of security and thus are lax in taking further measures to secure their property. That would be an extra layer of security.

I want to emphasize that I am not knocking alarm systems and I sincerely believe in them as part of a good defense against burglary, not to mention that they usually allow for insurance discounts to your homeowners or business policy. What you purchase for your home is a personal choice, one which you should feel addresses your particular needs or application. I only want to stress how important it is not to be entirely dependent on the alarm system by itself.

Video Systems

Probably one of the most talked about and advertised systems today is video. Today everyone with a cell phone is a walking camera capable of taking still pictures and/or video. Not to mention, anytime we go anywhere, there is sure to be a camera recording our every move. Add to that the technology of facial recognition and it really makes you think. When driving your car or shopping at the store or doing pretty much anything, a camera is in near proximity documenting you and your every move.

Let's cover video surveillance of your home/business. Whether part of a wireless burglar alarm app system or an independent hardwired system with internet connectivity, I'm sure most of you have seen all those fancy video systems available on the market today allowing you to access live video/pictures on your smart phone or tablet from wherever. Awesome, right?

My personal opinion is that video surveillance of your home/business is a good thing, not only as part of a good burglary prevention plan, but also as a means of checking on your loved ones or pets while you are away.

So many of my investigations gave me the opportunity to view video of the burglary after the fact, at times proving to be very useful to the investigation. But as with any part of a good burglary prevention plan, it's not the end all. Video only provides you with what the system has recorded and what a savvy burglar allows you to see. That's right. As I noted, many burglars watch the same television commercials and research the same products you do, if not more so. So, you can imagine they do whatever it takes to conceal their identity.

Miami Moon

I think this would be the perfect point
in which to tell you about the video I refer
to as, "The Miami Moon". In the course
of reviewing the security video of one of my

I think the best approach in helping you with the decision-making process of video systems, would be for me to share with you what I would look for as a detective when viewing burglary scene video.

First and foremost, I evaluate the clarity of the video footage, whether shot during the daytime or at night (infra-red). I can't tell you how many times I would respond to a burglary scene with video that fell far short of what would be considered not just acceptable footage, but video with prosecutorial value. This means that the quality of the video must be such that it can be shown in a court of law to help in securing a verdict of guilt. Therefore, the video has to provide evidence beyond any reasonable doubt. Many videos fall short of this threshold.

When utilizing video as a means of identifying the burglar, the image captured by the video camera has to be extremely clear. Any distortion of the image will render it of no value for a positive identification of the subject. I can't tell you how many prosecutors told me they would not be able to use the victim's video footage as it lacked the clarity or quality for prosecution. It is important for you to choose a system that not only provides a clear picture when viewing it in its standard format, but also maintains clarity when used to extract and enlarge still photos for identification. This translates into the system having a pixel count sufficient for this purpose!

The video footage should be able to confirm the exact time that the burglary occurred with a date/time stamp. This feature is standard to most systems. It is important that you maintain the proper date/time stamp. Many times, victims would inform me that the video I was viewing was actually off by an hour due to daylight savings time or the date/time had not been set as they "weren't good with electronics". If this is the case, seek help from the salesperson who sold you the system or ask the neighborhood geek to assist.

Next, how many subjects were involved and what were the actions of each of the subjects? This translates into having cameras positioned not only inside of your residence/business, and around the outside as well. Remember, NO BLIND SPOTS! Many times, I was disappointed to see that a burglar was able to walk off camera; meaning there were areas around the perimeter of the building that were out of view of the camera. This was often because the owner believed that a particular side of the building without entry/exit points was not important to cover. You never know when a burglar will let his/her guard down and expose a critical element that can be used for apprehension and prosecution purposes.

Also, I loved to see video footage that included the burglar's vehicle. This always proved to be a great investigative lead. Many cases were closed as a result of distributing a picture of the subject's vehicle to road patrol officers which led to investigative stops and identification of the subject.

Finally, my favorite videos were those which provided some unique feature of the subject(s). This could be a particular piece of clothing, whether a t-shirt or hat advertising some location, or a particular hair style that could be seen as unique. And, of course a subject's tattoo is always a great clue.

A Very Telling Tattoo

> *I was called to the scene of a commercial burglary of a restaurant. The burglar had entered the restaurant in the late-night hours by breaking the door glass. The burglar could not be identified by face on the video though did have a distinct tattoo on his left forearm that was clearly visible. I distributed a still photo of the subject's tattoo to the uniform patrol officers working that district. As it turned out, a couple of weeks later a patrol officer noticed a panel van driving suspiciously through a strip mall late at night after businesses hours. When the officer stopped the vehicle per officer safety protocol, he asked the driver to extend his hands out the driver's side window and there it was. The officer immediately saw that the driver had a tattoo matching that pictured in the bulletin I had distributed. I responded and interviewed the driver who soon confessed to the restaurant burglary as well as several others that had occurred earlier in the year.*

After reviewing a video, my final on scene responsibility was to recover the video for investigative and prosecutorial purposes. To this end, I relied heavily on the expertise of detectives that worked in the Forensic Video Services Unit. Detectives assigned to the unit are highly trained in all aspects of video systems and the protocol for the proper recovery and storage of crime scene video. This is done to maintain the highest degree of integrity of the video. The technology of video systems has to be respected. Forensic video detectives are also considered subject matter experts in their field and thus their testimony is well respected in court related filings, as well as rebuttal to challenges made by the defense to include the trial.

Video systems that make the recovery and/or storage of recordings fairly easy are preferred. This process is also dependent on the time period in which the video is stored in memory. Some systems can store a large amount of data before "recording over" what had been previously recorded a day, week or month ago. It may take a bit of time for a forensic detective or crime scene technician to respond and recover the video, so you must be certain to have a sufficient amount of data storage.

So, now that I have outlined a number of details that I look for in a burglary scene video, you have a starting point from which to start shopping for the right system. Remember that just as with alarm systems, there are a multitude of video systems touting to be the best. Take the time to research what system best fits your particular application whether residential or business. One last thought as you're going through your list of what you need with the salesperson, you may want to ask them how the system can be disabled. You might be surprised by the answer. Again, just a thought.

Storing Your Valuables

The storing of your valuables is one of the most important steps to your burglary awareness and prevention plan. I cannot stress this enough. The steps you take in the storage of your valuables can make the difference between a minor case, if there could ever be a minor case, and a major financial and personal loss.

One of the most fascinating things that I discovered over the years of investigating burglaries is the way people store their valuables. Working in Miami gave me the opportunity to serve people from all walks of life and cultures. Though no matter how different in race, color or creed, ninety-nine percent of victims all stored their valuables in the same place; their master bedroom. And of course, ninety-nine percent of the burglars I arrested knew that as well.

As I noted earlier in the typical burglary, once burglars gain entry to your home, they immediately look for the master bedroom. Once there they will ransack the room in search of your most valued possessions. Most experienced burglars, especially those who are career criminals, know that the master bedroom is where they will find the most value for their effort.

Think of it. Your home is your castle, but your master bedroom is your sanctuary and location most private to you; O.K., so man caves aside. This is a part of your home that visitors, friends or even relatives are generally not welcome. For this very reason the master bedroom is generally where we store all of our most valued of possessions whether jewelry, cash, cameras, laptops, tablets, cell phones, firearms, collectables or that special something that you don't want the kids to get or play with. It's all in the master bedroom. Remember when talking about alarm systems I mentioned that the control box for your alarm containing all of the wiring and phone connections is usually in the, you got it, master bedroom closet. Burglars will access the alarm box in an attempt to disable your alarm. Sometimes ripping the entire box off the wall and causing a great deal of structural damage as well. Finally, we all love to think we are being smart in having a safe in the master bedroom/closet.

So, need I say more. You need to be a bit more creative and find alternate locations for the storage of your valuables. This is an area where entrepreneurs have found a way to make money offering a wide range of products that are for storing your valuables ranging from safes to containers that give the appearance of being something else, such as the infamous hollowed book. Of course, I have to mention the fake rock that holds a key to your home placed in close proximity to the front door.

I will cover safes in greater detail in just a bit. But for now, let's talk about what may be the best alternative and something a bit more practical for every day.

I believe the best approach to storing valuables is to first determine and separate those valuables that you use on a daily basis versus those you may just use every once in a while. For example, you probably don't wear those family heirlooms (jewels) that were handed down to you to work every day. Or perhaps you keep some emergency cash in your nightstand drawer just for a rainy day. By separating these valuables, you can now find alternate locations by which to store (hide) them around the home. I'm a big supporter of placing jewelry and personal documents (i.e., birth certificates, passports, social security cards, marriage certificates etc.) in a safe deposit box at your local bank. I would liken this philosophy to the old saying, don't put all your eggs in one basket. Many burglars said they would commonly see many of these personal documents lying around though identity theft wasn't their thing. I can tell you that passports are a hot commodity in burglaries. Finally, you should consider where to store your checkbook.

My Wife's Rice Cooker

I would like to share another story with you that comes to mind. I remember speaking with my wife one day about finding alternate hiding places to put valuables. My wife suggested that an old rice cooker we had was the best place for us to hide certain valuables. You see my wife is of Cuban descent and any Cuban worth their salt will tell you that a rice and pressure cooker are staples in a kitchen. Actually, it was perfect as I couldn't recall a case where a burglar had searched the kitchen appliances for valuables. For many years to follow our rice cooker would double as a safe.

Later in the book I'm going to address maintaining an inventory of your possessions (valuables). I would suggest that as you put together your inventory, this would be the ideal time to evaluate where items should be stored.

The principle idea is to not store all of your valuables in the master bedroom, thus reducing the impact/loss in the event of an actual break-in. I can't tell you how many victims have lost valuables, mainly jewelry, in a matter of a few minutes as it was stored in a jewelry box located in the master bedroom. Once taken, the monetary value is secondary to the sentimental value. Given all the advice that I provide in this book, please take to heart this one thing that will make a huge difference in the outcome of a burglary.

Safes

In continuing the discussion of storing your valuables, safes are one of the more commonly used vehicles in which to store valuables and perhaps the most misunderstood as well. I will tell you that in my experience only on a very few occasions did a safe live up to its purpose in protecting a person's valuables. This was not always due to a particular defect of the product though due to the use and/or application by which a victim depended on it.

I feel the best approach for determining what type and/or size of safe is right for you first depends on what you wish to store in the safe and for what purpose. Basic questions would be whether you wish to use the safe for the storage of valuables such as jewelry, or do you require a larger safe that would accommodate firearms (pistols and/or long guns).

Safes are generally given a rating both in terms of being resistant to burglary/theft and resistant to fire. Obviously, when storing valuable documents, you may be more concerned about the fire rating of the safe for the preservation of the documents in the event of fire. It would be advisable that you research these ratings and any reviews relating to the safe you are considering for your needs.

Another consideration would be whether a stand-alone (above ground) safe or a floor safe is best for your particular application.

Going back to investigations, very few safes lived up to my victims' expectations. This was mainly because they had gone out and purchased a safe and placed it where? Of course, most times in the master bedroom closet. Location was only one issue, the other being that the safe was not properly installed. For example, in the case of a stand-alone safe that was bolted to the floor, many people did not use the proper hardware (bolts) to secure the safe to the floor which made it extremely easy for the burglar to use a pry bar to pop the safe from its anchored position. I handled many cases in which this was the case. I would strongly encourage you to consult with a professional when considering where and how to best install the particular safe you have chosen.

A Safe That Wasn't Secure(d)

I remember responding to the scene of a residential burglary and as I stepped inside the front door of the residence, I noticed a set of tracks carved into the floor tile of the home. It turned out that the burglars had stolen a very large and heavy gun safe from the home and literally dragged it, its legs scouring the tile floor enroute, from its location to the front door of the residence. After having dragged the safe to the doorway, the evidence showed that the burglars had backed a pick-up truck up to the front door in order to load the safe. So, evidently the preferred method in dealing with safes was not to "crack" the safe at the scene of the crime as seen on TV, but to just take the safe altogether to a location where the burglars could take their time to open it by whatever means.

I believe one of the best safes you could have, particularly for storing smaller items and/or documents, is a floor safe. This type of safe is installed into the sub-floor of your home set in concrete and can easily be concealed. Being properly installed, it is virtually almost impossible to remove from its position without taking a lot of time and with the use of some heavy tools, just what a burglar does not want to deal with.

Now let's focus on businesses that commonly utilize a safe to store cash among other valuables such as business records, check books and the like. Business owners need to first be aware that a safe can be defeated by a burglar either by removing the safe in its entirety from the business or simply opening it on site. Now not all burglars are safe crackers per se; though many burglars have employed cutting a safe open with any number of tools or a torch. You see, burglars that break into your business have a lot more time to execute the burglary than a typical residential home. I have seen many cases in which the crime scene or surveillance video showed that the burglar in some cases had taken hours to accomplish the theft. This is something to think about when considering the rating of the safe you purchase.

Additionally, I would like to bring to your attention how much cash you wish to store in your business safe. I would suggest this amount to be only as much as is required in order to open for the following day of business, with the exception of a small amount of coin for change. Any additional amount of cash beyond that is unnecessarily at risk of being stolen.

Many of the safe jobs that I handled as a detective involved the burglar having prior knowledge of the amounts of cash being stored. Typically, some businesses would store bank deposits over a weekend for example until the owner and/or manager returned on Monday morning to physically make a bank deposit. Burglars told me that this information provided the incentive to execute the crime. Many burglars said they would not bother to burglarize a business that held little or no cash. Now that's not to say that it doesn't happen. What I am suggesting is just another layer of prevention.

Another option (to avoid holding large amounts of cash in the safe) would be to make regular deposits at your bank. Businesses are able to make deposits at all hours via a drop box. This box is generally located in the drive-thru of the bank and doesn't require the customer to exit their vehicle. This is just an alternative and something to consider depending on the operational needs of your business.

Finally, should the cash register of your business be visible through the front window of the business, it would be best to either remove the cash drawer from the register or at least leave it in an open position giving the indication that no cash is present. Some businesses will post signage on the window indicating that no cash is kept on the premises.

Again, as with anything discussed within this book, I strongly suggest you do your own research and decide what best serves your application.

Pets… Everyone's Best Friend

Pets are one of my favorite topics in burglary awareness and prevention. Personally, my wife and I have a dog and two birds. What a team. We love our pets, and should you have pets of your own, I'm sure you know what I mean. Pets take a unique place in our life and heart. There are all kinds of stories out there about how a hero pet saved the life of its owner by some amazing feat or another.

With all the gadgets and technology out there, I found that one of the best things people could have to prevent a break-in was a pet, or more specifically a large dog. Now I don't want to seem prejudicial for or against any particular type of pet or breed, but if I had to actually count how many burglaries I investigated in which the victim had a large dog standing guard, I could probably count them all on one or maybe two hands.

Pets Sounding the Alarm

When discussing pets and their deterrent value, I'm reminded of a case my unit handled involving a residence that doubled as a fencing operation. A fencing operation being a location where stolen property is exchanged for cash/drugs. We secured a search warrant for the residence and enlisted the assistance of the Special Response Team (SWAT) to execute the warrant given the high risk of the operation.

Upon executing the search warrant the Special Response Team made entry to secure the residence as was protocol. I was positioned at the front of the residence as we made entry and could hear the Team utilizing flashbangs (flash/percussion grenades used to temporarily disorient offenders/threats).

What I saw next was both unexpected and unnerving. A full-grown male wolf; yes, a huge wolf came charging out of the front door of the residence. This was unusual even for Miami. With my firearm drawn, I kept aim on the wolf as he was at full charge out of the home. I quickly realized that he wasn't charging me though more than likely just frightened by the grenade and in his own hurry to leave. Not so lucky were two pit bulls that charged the entry team which had to be put down.

After clearing the residence, I discovered two Scarlet Macaws in an aviary at the rear of the residence. They were beautiful birds and LOUD. Undoubtedly being used as an alarm. Yes, birds are uniquely alert to their surroundings and approaching strangers, causing them to squawk loudly.

Later in the evening, the wolf returned to the residence and was hesitant to get near any of us. We decided he was hungry for dinner, so we fed him an entire roast chicken. No Big Macs.

When interviewing burglary subjects, I would ask about dogs. The responses were quite amazing. As it turned out, almost all of the subjects I discussed this topic with told me they were either afraid of big dogs or felt that dogs were too much trouble to deal with.

Some did mention taking pets for profit. Most often young pets such as puppies or kittens. Mostly purebred animals. These pets could then be sold easily on the street or in flea markets. I can recall several heart-breaking cases in which victims suffered the theft of their dog.

On A Sad Note

One case in particular was of a puppy that was ill and required medication. The victim was totally overcome with sadness and worry that her puppy was going to die without the meds. Clearly the burglar(s) had taken the dog without the knowledge that the dog required medication in order to survive. My only hope was that perhaps the burglars would have eventually realized that the puppy required medical attention and taken him to a local veterinarian. I distributed flyers with a photograph of the pup hoping for a break in the case though to no avail.

My only suggestion to avoid this type of situation would be to place your pets that may be vulnerable or requiring special attention and/or medication, in a day care facility when away from home.

A common question is whether or not your dog would be poisoned by a burglar. Let me tell you that I can't recall one case where the burglar poisoned the victim's pet, waiting for the poison to take effect and then committing the crime. It never happened. Remember time is of the essence for the burglar. In all honesty I have more often encountered cases in which the burglar confined the victim's dog to a certain location of the home, be it in one of the bedrooms, the garage or outside. To be even more clear, these were cases in which the dogs were usually not a large breed.

The theft of exotic birds and reptiles is also very popular. Let me share a few cases with you.

Rosie's Ransom

Rosie was an exotic parrot who had been stolen from the victim's residence and held for ransom. That's right, the bad guy took Rosie and subsequently contacted the victim and demanded $1000.00 for her return. The victim advised that the subject wanted to meet at an undisclosed location and exchange Rosie for the cash. My squad coordinated with the Crime Suppression Team, a plain-clothes undercover unit, to assist in "Operation Rosie". We had the victim communicate with the subject and convince him that she wanted to get Rosie back without the police getting involved. A meeting was set, and the Crime Suppression Team surveilled the location. In short order, the subject was identified and arrested. And yes, we recovered Rosie and she was reunited with her owner.

Old Oscar

In another case, the burglar stole an amazon parrot by the name of Oscar. Oscar had been with the family for eighteen years.

Needless to say, his theft was devastating to the entire family, many of which were in tears, as they had lost a "family member." It was a heart wrenching investigation. Two days after the burglary we made an arrest in another case that led to Oscar's recovery. The burglars had intended to sell Oscar at a flea market. Needless to say, Oscar's family was overjoyed by his return.

Reptile Rip

Lastly, in one particular case, an exotic one, the victim's snakes were the target. This was a unique and very interesting case in which the victim was a snake enthusiast and breeder. He had a large number of exotic snakes from all around the world. In a unique twist, a breeder from Georgia who was aware of the victim's collection, hired a burglar to break into the victim's residence in Miami and steal the snakes. The objective was to transport the snakes to Georgia where they were destined for breeding and the black market. The case turned into a multi-agency effort of both local and federal agencies, ending in the arrest of the subjects and recovery of the snakes.

Quick Note

An interesting tidbit of information is that the contraband most smuggled into the United States, other than narcotics, is of exotic reptiles and animals.

In addition to pets being a benefit to protecting your home or business, there is companionship. Pets are great companions offering unconditional love to their owners which in turn gives owners a sense of security. This is especially true for children in the home. I would encourage everyone to strongly consider buying, or better yet, adopting a pet as a wonderful addition to any family. Have you ever visited a shelter? You would be amazed at the number of beautiful pets that are in need of someone to love them and give them a good home. I should mention that it really doesn't cost much either. Another benefit is that you can rest assured that you are getting a healthy pet that has been given a complete medical exam and all of the required inoculations. Consider this another layer of prevention.

A final thought, should you have a dog or cat that is allowed to exit or enter the residence via a dog door, you may want to consider having a means by which to secure the door against intrusion. This is just one of those big little details that we tend to overlook when protecting the home.

Crime Prevention Through Environmental Design (CPTED)

Crime prevention through environmental design or commonly referred to as CPTED, is a very important component of a burglary awareness and prevention plan. CPTED, as related to residential and commercial burglaries, deals primarily with the creation of an environment that would deter the criminal from the commission of the crime, whether physically or psychologically. This is accomplished by combining natural elements with man-made structures and technology around the exterior of the structure.

I know you're probably asking yourself what does all this mean? Simply put, I want you to picture your home or business in your mind as I put CPTED in its simplest terms. You see, when prowling neighborhoods, most burglars told me how they picked a certain home or business to burglarize simply by the "look" of the location which in turn gave them a "feeling" of either comfort or discomfort. Simply put, picturing your home or business, do you think it's inviting to a burglar? CPTED addresses this question.

Many police departments offer some form of community service concerning burglary prevention tips to include CPTED principles. In fact, many community service officers attend specialized training to become CPTED certified. You may want to check if your local police department offers this program.

Let us first address what CPTED principles may help you prevent your home from being targeted for a burglary. Again, when discussing these principles, I would like you to picture yourself standing directly in front of your home, as seen from the eyes of the public or more specifically, the burglar. What do you see? Remember we want to create a scene that deters burglars both physically and psychologically. Your home may have a barred door and windows, steel reinforced front door and frame, hurricane or impact resistant glass windows, signage indicating the home is protected by an alarm system and landscaping such as thorny plants strategically placed by windows, though not to offer concealment to a would-be burglar. You may have fencing around your home with gated entry or perhaps you may have installed video surveillance cameras. And of course, strategically placed lighting for night time hours.

If you are a business owner, you may consider further measures such as roll down shutters that secure the entire store front and/or concrete pillars placed along the store frontage to deter forced entry by vehicles being used as battering rams to enter a building.

Perhaps there is an emphasis on protecting what we in the police department would consider entry/exit points of a structure. In the following segment I will address the physical/structural barriers in more detail.

As we discussed aspects of the CPTED model for your home or business you should be better equipped to identify where you might consider making some changes to create that environment which has both physical and psychological deterrent value. Hence, reducing the chances of being burglarized.

Structural Barriers

Structural barriers as related to burglary are those structural/ physical points throughout a residence or business which shield the structure from entry. Having structural barriers can, and have, made the difference between a burglary having been committed or merely attempted, as in no entry gained.

I mentioned a number of physical (structural) barriers in the CPTED segment of this book. Now I would like to address some in a little more detail as related to cases I investigated over the years.

I liken structural barriers to layers of protection that have to be overcome by the burglar in order that he/she is able to make entry to a building. Let's say we have a home that is enclosed by a fence and beyond that fence the home has bars over the windows and/or front door. Beyond that, the windows are impact resistant and the door is steel reinforced. Even further, the door may have more than one locking mechanism, whether it be a simple deadbolt or one of the higher tech security locks. I'm sure you can understand the concept.

Before you run out and start buying fences, security bars, steel doors, locks and new impact windows, let me remind you that a chain is only as strong as its weakest link. Not to mention, it can get very expensive and nothing is a 100% sure thing.

Let's start at the top with fences. Fences come in all shapes and sizes and in my experience are a good first line of defense. The only thing I would caution you on is that those fences which are so-called "privacy fences," those which one cannot see through, can act against you as well. Many burglars like the fact that once they overcome (climb over) a privacy fence, the same privacy you enjoy while lounging in your backyard is now privacy for the burglar to enter your home without being seen.

Next, I'll address security bars. Most people would think that security bars are a great way to keep unwanted guests out, although they may tend to look a little unappealing to the eye; covering all of your windows and doors along the exterior of your residence. I'm sure there are those of you that value a greater sense of security over style. At least that is what burglary victims have told me. Anyway, you be the judge. I believe that first and foremost one needs to feel secure in your home. Let me just share a story with you.

A False Sense of Security

> *I investigated a string of burglaries committed to homes, all of which had security bars. The investigation revealed that the method used to defeat the security bars was identical in all of the cases, indicating they were all committed by the same individual. As it turned out, I arrested an individual who confessed to all of the burglaries and his occupation was that of installing security bars for a Miami area company. The subject told me that he obviously knew how to defeat the bars given his profession and felt that the victims whom had installed the bars, 'had a false sense of security', thus leaving valuables out and about for the taking. Again, nothing is a 100%.*

Next, I would like to talk about impact resistant (hurricane) windows for your home. As I mentioned in the Commercial Burglary chapter of this book, these windows, depending on the manufacturer, are built to sustain winds of up to 200 mph and the flying debris that comes with that. All I can say is that these windows are awesome though very expensive. I have seen countless videos of burglars attempting to break an impact resistant window to no avail. It's almost comical to see the persistence of a burglar striking a window or door repeatedly and becoming more and more frustrated with every swing or kick. It's usually more likely that the door or window framing break before the impact resistant glass.

A surveillance video from a residential burglary that I investigated shows two juvenile males approach the master bedroom sliding glass doors made of impact glass. One of the juveniles then produced a common burglary tool used to break glass that I should refrain from describing as this is not a training manual for burglars. He began to strike the window with the tool to no avail. Frustrated with this, the juvenile began to kick the door glass, at one comical point falling back onto his a-- (back side). Determined to break the glass, the juvenile then picked up a brick he found in the victim's yard which was part of a landscape design feature. He again gave it his all, as if a major league pitcher, throwing the brick with all his might and striking the door glass at center. NO LUCK. Needless to say, this young man had to abandon the idea of breaking the glass and his attempt to enter the residence all together.

The only advise I would share with you is that you research the various types of impact resistant windows in today's market and decide what fits your particular application and budget.

Addressing the topic of locks, first let me say that the percentage of lock-pick burglaries is very small. True "lock pick" burglars are far and few between. Far more prevalent would be the bump lock burglar who uses a key, referred to as a bump key to defeat the locking mechanism. Again, depending on your feelings on the matter you may want to look into higher end locks that have proven to be more resistant to being picked or even consider a keyless lock system.

So, let me finish this segment with doors. Now when we talk about doors there are many types to consider. I will highlight just those that stand out for me as related to the burglaries I investigated.

When thinking about doors I'm sure the first thing that comes to your mind is your front door. A very common type of burglary is a door kick. This is pretty self-explanatory. The burglar is looking for a door that has the appearance of being easy to defeat with just one swift kick along the lock side of the door. This tends to be quite successful when dealing with a common or standard wood door and frame. The result is damage to not only the door, but the frame as well. The remedy that I would suggest to you is to have a steel door with steel reinforced framing. The added strength and support of the door generally exponentially increases its strength and resistance against forced entry.

Some other types of doors to discuss are those of all glass and/or having glass inserts. Some burglars have told me that they like glass doors as they offer a "line of sight" into the residence. Not to mention that many can be easily defeated by simply breaking out the glass.   Should your door be all glass it would be advisable to make sure that it is constructed with impact resistant material. Should you have glass inserts either in the door or alongside of the door, consider impact glass as well. Which reminds me… I have seen many cases of glass inserts being broken allowing the burglar access to reach inside and unlock the door. So, if your door has a deadbolt lock with a key access on the interior, instead of a latch, please don't leave the key in the lock.

Now let's talk about sliding glass doors. These are probably the number one type of door that burglars tend to focus on. Why? Simply put, it is generally easy to defeat by either breaking the glass or lifting it from its track. As well many homes have a number of sliding glass doors at the rear of the residence where the burglar is less likely to be seen or heard. Again, I would suggest if you have a sliding glass door that you consider the impact resistant glass. Also, a quick visit to the hardware store will reveal a multitude of products that are easy for you to install that secure the door from being lifted off its track.

So, there you have it. You should now have a pretty good understanding of structural barriers, though more importantly, how you can design them to work against an intrusion.

Crime Watch and Your Neighbors

The topic of Crime Watch and your neighbors is really one of great importance for burglary awareness and prevention. Your neighborhood and neighbors are an extension of your home or business. Having a relationship with those whom live and work around you is of great value in so many ways. In this segment I will touch on one of the most successful programs available to citizens most anywhere. That program being your NEIGHBORHOOD CRIME WATCH.

My first exposure to Neighborhood Crime Watch was when I was asked by the Community Service Unit of my department to give a presentation about burglary to the members (residents) of a local Crime Watch. I should add that the residents lived in an area that was also under a homeowner's association (HOA). This was an awesome experience for me to witness a group of citizens coming together to address common problems within the neighborhood. Leading the meeting was the Neighborhood Crime Watch coordinator for Miami-Dade County with support from my departments Community Service Unit and of course myself, representing the Burglary Unit. My participation in this presentation is actually what sparked the birth of this book.

The basic concept of a Neighborhood Crime Watch is the partnership and participation of neighbors for one common goal, crime prevention. Now that seems so simplistic though it actually works. You get your neighbors together, whether it's a potluck dinner or just a simple gathering where you agree to be each other's eyes and ears for the neighborhood. As you fellowship with others you have now become involved in something of great value. I'm not just talking about burglary prevention. I'm talking about the endless opportunities that come from interacting with and getting to know others. I've seen folks develop many other relationships whether business, babysitting or yes even love, that have come from a Crime Watch.

A typical Neighborhood Crime Watch group appoints someone as a Block Captain who will liaison with the local police department and be able to organize monthly meetings and disseminate information to the residents. In an HOA, this may be someone on the board of directors who can incorporate Crime Watch news and events within the HOA newsletter. A current telephone and/or email list would also be maintained so as to have up to date contact information for residents.

Meetings, usually held on a monthly basis or at least quarterly, are designed to inform you about current crime trends and statistics in your area. I would generally attend meetings equipped with a burglary statistical report that was generated by the Crime Analysis Unit. The report would cover not only how many residential and/or vehicle burglaries had occurred in the area, though also information on subject and/or suspicious vehicles that had been reported in the area. Again, the sharing of this information would sometimes prove key to solving cases.

I coined the words partnership and participation in this segment because without either, the whole concept will not work and will ultimately fall apart. One must not only be in partnership by attending the meetings but must also participate by being capable of reacting when you see something that seems out of sorts. I would always tell victims and witnesses alike; you know it in your knower. Let me caution you that participation or reacting does not mean taking action, as in, confronting anyone acting suspiciously or placing yourself in harm's way. The idea is simply to observe and report. More than likely you will be given a short tutorial at a Crime Watch meeting on how to properly report your observations i.e. subject and/ or vehicle descriptions and their respective actions. Crime watch is not a vigilante organization.

I can't tell you how many times I have interviewed witnesses of burglaries whom have seen the entire burglary unfolding before their very eyes and felt something was wrong, though they neglected to call the police.

A Hesitant Neighbor

A witness once told me she saw a pick-up truck backed into her neighbor's (the victim's) driveway and watched as three teenage boys loaded the truck with items from the home. The witness said that although she was suspicious, she hesitated in calling the police because she knew the neighbor had teenage children and thus dismissed the event as perhaps friends helping out. Of course, the three teenagers were in fact burglars and had stolen the neighbor's jewelry, game system and wide screen TV.

If that witness had been a member of the Neighborhood Crime Watch, at the very least, she would have been able to call and check on her neighbor. If unable to reach her neighbor, she would have known to call the police.

Some of you might be thinking that you don't want your neighbors getting involved in your private life. That is not what I'm talking about or what Crime Watch is about. You are simply involved in a network of neighbors who are just watching out for each other. I would strongly suggest looking into it and if not already established in your neighborhood, contact your local police department. One indication of an already established Crime Watch in your area would be Crime Watch signage at the entrances to your neighborhood or HOA.

I figured this would be the best segment in which to also mention going on vacation as it has a lot to do with the ability to have someone looking after your home while your away. Having a Crime Watch neighbor watch over your home can help ease your mind. Another thing you could do is let your Community Service Unit officer know your departure and return dates. And finally, please don't post your vacation plans on social media.

The Miami-Dade Police Department typically generates a Watch Order. The Watch Order will be assigned to uniform patrol officers in your area and will list effective dates and purpose of the order i.e., vacation or suspicious activity and your address and personal information to include any vehicles you will be leaving parked at the location. Typically, officers are required to periodically check the watch order location and document the date/time of the check. Check with the Crime Watch or Community Service officer in your area to see if they have something similar in practice.

In closing, I would encourage you to look into your Neighborhood Crime Watch or at the very least, get to know a neighbor or two. It might be the best thing you ever did.

Education and Having a Plan

One of the most important segments of this entire book is education and planning. If you follow no other advice, I would hope for you to take to heart this topic which I consider to be the most important. In this segment I will cover what I believe to be sound procedures for you and your family to put into practice when faced with the threat of a burglary.

Remember that my entire objective is to share with you every aspect of what I have had to deal with at one point or another over the course of my career as related to burglary. In order to accomplish this objective, I cannot ignore the possibility that you may come face to face with an in-progress burglary. That is to ask, what would you do if a burglar comes to your door or enters your home while you and/or your children are present?

Without sounding overly dramatic, over the years I have seen many families suffer terrible things that could have easily been avoided with the proper education and planning. In most cases, to no fault of the parents, children are those most affected as they are inherently alone at home waiting for their parents to return from work. And let me qualify children as those of a mature age, fully capable of caring for themselves absent any parent or guardian. I have dealt with many burglaries that were committed while a child was at home alone awaiting a parent to return.

Today we live in a society whereby parents, whether single or married, work tirelessly to support their family. Most work a 9 to 5 job and that doesn't include the commute. Many children are required to return home from school and care for themselves until joined by a parent or guardian. Perhaps a child is ill and left at home to rest or home for spring break or summer vacation while parents are still required to go to work.

I am emphasizing the issue of children who find themselves home alone because as I have said, the majority of residential burglaries are committed during daytime hours. So, in other words, should it be your misfortune to be the victim of a burglary, knowing that odds are it will occur during the day while you are working, and your children are at home, what will happen? Have your children been educated on how to handle a break-in, a fire or any emergency for that matter? Does your family have a plan?

I have put together some basics for you on how to react when faced with a burglary. The focus will be on everything from a mere unexpected knock at the door to the realization that someone is trying to get into your home or has already gained entry and is in some area of the house with you. Given these basics, you and your family will be better equipped to develop a plan based on your particular circumstances. I have formulated these basics over the years based on investigations and interviews of burglars who were willing to share their thoughts on what they were looking for and/or doing in the course of committing burglaries. It was surprising to see a commonality between burglars in what they look for and how they felt about interacting with victims.

As I have previously noted, most burglars don't want to enter a home while it is occupied. Burglars are generally focused on being able to enter without confronting a victim or animal (pet), for that matter. Not to mention that in the State of Florida the commission of an occupied burglary carries an enhanced penalty by law. Most all burglars take steps to ensure that a residence is unoccupied. The most common way to accomplish this is to simply knock at the door to see if anyone answers. This is very important to you as your response will determine whether the subject leaves the residence or proceeds with breaking into the home.

There are many of you who don't like answering the door to unexpected guests. I get it. Also, parents typically instruct their children not to answer or open the door for anyone. So now given the fact that we know almost all burglars like to ring your doorbell or knock before committing the burglary, we know that your response is critical. Should there be no response given, the burglar's next step is to make entry. I have responded to many cases where that was exactly what happened, and I arrived to find a child crying and distraught over this terrifying experience.

Burglars Are Wise to Tricks

> *A quick thought that just came to mind,*
> *don't think that just because you leave a TV*
> *or stereo on with the volume up the burglar*
> *will leave. Most burglars say that they know*
> *about that trick and are not fooled.*

So, here are some responses you may consider. When a stranger knocks at the door, instruct your children to yell out, "Mom/ Dad someone's at the door." Now the burglar can hear that #1, the home is occupied, and #2, children and a parent(s) are present. I suggest this response be repeated to assure being heard. Yell out, "Mom/Dad get the door. I'm playing my game(video)." Or another response such as, "Mom/Dad get the door. I'm on the phone." This will let the burglar know that there is someone on the telephone with your child and therefore has the ability to call the police should something happen. Along with this vocal response your child should call the police (911). That's right don't be shy. Call the police. Your children should advise the complaint officer that they are home alone, and a stranger is at the door. In some cases, depending on the layout of your home, you child may be able to see the stranger, or a vehicle. It is important that they provide a description of both to the best of their ability. Given that most children have their own cell phone today in day, they should take a picture of the stranger and vehicle if safe to do so.

Now realize I said to call the police (911) first. Minutes and seconds count when dealing with a possible crime in progress. I would tell victims that I would rather be called to a thousand false calls than know that I wasn't called to the one that counted. I have responded to many in progress burglaries too late, to our detriment, because children thought or were told they should call their parents first. In many cases it was the parent on the line with the complaint desk relaying information as they were on the other line with their children. This can be a dangerous situation for all. It causes all kinds of problems not being able to speak directly with the person (victim) on scene.

The resolve to this issue is simple. Educate your children on how to call the police. I know many parents already have discussed the concept of calling 911 for help though I suggest taking this to another level. Conduct scenario training to reinforce the lesson. The whole family can participate in conducting drills covering the scenarios that I have listed. When placed in a stressful situation, remembering what you were told to do can easily be forgotten without prior training and reinforcement. Scenario training helps commit your mind and body to what action should be taken.

Should telephone communication be a problem, a good alternative of notifying the police that you are in need of assistance would be to activate the panic alarm function of your alarm system. Remember what I told you about alarms. A panic alarm will prioritize the police response. Of course, this will require that your children have a working knowledge of your home alarm system aside from just knowing the code to the alarm.

I have thus far focused on children responding to a stranger at the door. What about you or your significant other? Adults should have a plan as well. Men and woman alike should make an effort to give the appearance that there is more than one person to deal with in the home. As for woman, I tell them to yell out in their most profound voice, "Joe, someone's at the door. Get the door." Followed by, "Joe, I told you to get the door. I'm busy." Don't be afraid of sounding too aggressive. That's the idea. You want the person on the other side of the door to know you're not a shy or frail person. As for the men, I would suggest you yell out, "Hey Jane, someone's at the door. Can you get it?" Followed by, "Jane, I'm on the phone, see who's at the door."

Many burglary subjects have told me that as soon as they knew that someone was home, they wasted no time in leaving. Those who actually made contact with the homeowner be it through the door or face to face, would ask for a friend by name or pretend they were looking for a landscaping job or their lost dog. Should this happen to you, beware. My advice would be that once you realize that the contact didn't feel right, "knowing it in your knower", call the police and let them know there is a suspicious person in your neighborhood. Remember they will want a physical description of the person (race, sex, height, weight, hair color and clothing worn) as well as any additional information, such as a vehicle description.

The Witness Who Claimed to Be an Artist

Speaking of being able to identify the subject of a crime brings to mind an exceptionally funny story of a case handled by one of the detectives in my unit. A witness to the burglary had informed the detective that he had seen the burglar and was positive that he could identify the subject. The detective of course asked if the witness could then describe the burglar. The witness responded by saying that he not only could describe the subject, in fact he had gotten such a good look at him he could sketch a drawing of him. The detective advised the witness he would

*welcome a drawing if he was so inclined and
provided a fax number by which to send the
drawing. Sure enough, the witness forwarded
his sketch of the subject he so adamantly felt
able to describe and draw. It was a sketch of
a stick person. True story.*

Now let us cover what to do if a burglar is actually attempting to gain entry to your home. You may see the burglar in the back yard looking for a point of entry or even prying at a window of your residence. First Call 911. Relay as much information as possible to the complaint officer while keeping yourself safe from harm's way. The complaint officer will guide you in this effort and immediately have the police on the way.

You may want to seek a safe way to exit the home. You don't want a confrontation. Should you be unable to exit the residence, find a room within the home to lock yourself in i.e. the bathroom. I know that some homes have what is referred to as a safe room. This is typically a custom-built room somewhat hidden within the residence. Of course, while doing this, you will continue to be on the phone with the police until police officers arrive.

Another scenario would be you returning home to find a burglar in your residence. Basically, the same principles apply. Call 911 and seek an immediate exit avoiding confrontation.

Should you or your children unavoidably find yourselves in the presence of a burglar, be as passive in nature as possible. More than likely their only concern will be one of escape. Most burglars are more afraid of interaction than you'd think. Remember most every burglar is only interested in stealing your valuables. They generally don't want to hurt anyone. In my experience, most assaults on victims occurred as result of the victim initiating some sort of confrontation. I have dealt with victims that act out in anger and attempt to apprehend the burglar on their own. This can and has led to the victim being injured. Again, a passive approach is best and to allow the police to pursue an apprehension.

One scenario that I have not covered would be an armed confrontation. This could mean that either the burglar or the victim is armed with a firearm or some other type of weapon. As for victims and their firearms, I will be addressing this topic in more detail later in the book. As for burglars being armed, I can only say that in my experience, burglars seldom arm themselves to commit a burglary. Now that is not to say that they don't steal firearms found in the home. In the State of Florida, a burglar who is armed or steals a firearm while in the commission of a burglary, has committed an armed burglary. Armed burglary carries severe penalties and is classified as a non-bondable offense. Funny enough, it is the NO BOND part of that offense that really gets the burglar's attention.

Should you encounter a burglar brandishing a firearm, try to avoid any action that would further aggravate the subject. Should escape not be an option, being passive and complying with demands would be the safest course of action. Carefully listen to and observe the burglar. This will help you in your response.

Quick Note

As a hostage negotiator I utilized listening as one of my most effective tools. You can tell many things by just listening to someone. Again, my grandmother used to say, "If your lips are moving, you're NOT listening." Voice and tone are very telling.

There are a million scenarios though all would begin with trying to maintain some sort of composure. Let me again reassure you that this type of confrontation would be extremely rare. Again, 99% of burglars want to avoid you and avoid the happenstance of you meeting each other

Now that I have covered these scenarios and possible responses, I would suggest that you and your family have a discussion and formulate a plan that best suits your situation. I'm sure the discussion of these scenarios alone will bring with it a better awareness of what we hope never occurs

After developing a plan, practice it by rehearsing each scenario. It could actually be fun for the family to share and even switch roles as you rehearse. The whole process is sure to be inspiring to all. Also, please understand that in any stressful situation we tend to forget the discussions and will tend to "freeze" in fear. Only by repetitive practice of your plan will you commit what you practiced to your subconscious and attain what I refer to as "muscle memory" and with it the ability to overcome the situation.

Social Media

Today in day I would be remiss in my efforts not to cover Social Media and the effect it can have on you as it relates to burglary and other crimes as well. Social media platforms are the most prolific websites and/or applications on the internet connecting billions of people.

People interact and enjoy the wonders of technology, as they have the ability to send each other instant messages, short videos of themselves and photographs of their breakfast, lunch and dinner. Personal interaction yields to a techno world that allows people to link with each other via an array of social media sites.

As people interact with friends, family and the world, they are also surrendering information. Information that those in the criminal world want and need in order to be successful in executing their crime(s).

As you message and send photos/videos your simultaneously in real time sharing information such as your location. That's right! Whether you realize it or not the social media platforms have something called a geotag. It's data, a digital media file, that pinpoints where you are physically located at any point in time. This is the kind of information criminals pine for.

So, as you send selfies' and messages to friends/family think about what you are sending to a criminal. For example, a burglar might learn that you are away from home on vacation. I can recall a case in which that occurred. The problem wasn't the friend/ family though someone that had friended or was following someone. Friending/following on the internet doesn't necessarily mean the person is your buddy, it basically is a list of people on the internet that are connected or linked to each other like a chain. You are thus unwittingly communicating to many whom you may not even know.

In the burglary case to which I refer, a teenage son of the victim had messaged about being away on vacation. A burglar (friend/ follower) took advantage of that information to break into the home without fear.

Other examples of social media platform sharing would be your eagerness to show friends photos of your new jewelry. Perhaps while posing with it in a selfie. Or maybe you are sharing photos of yourself, or your home, wherein the background of the photo you're revealing something better kept private. I once viewed a video whereby in the background I happened to notice the location of the persons safe. This would be a teaser for a burglar.
Placing the shoe on the other foot many criminals, to the advantage of the police, have posted photos/videos better kept private as well.

The Nike Burglar

I investigated a burglary in which the burglar took a pair of Nike sneakers from the victim. Now this pair of Nikes' weren't just your common Nike's. The sneakers had been custom made for the victim by Nike. Thus, the sneakers were "one of a kind".

The burglar in a pretentious display decided to post the shoes he had acquired (stolen) on social media. As it turned out a friend of a friend on social media alerted the victim that he had undoubtedly seen his Nike's posted.

*I was immediately contacted and told
of the discovery. After securing a subpoena
I made contact with the burglar and he
confessed to the burglary and the Nike's were
recovered as well as other property stolen in
the burglary.*

Gang Banger Stars

*In another story a gang banger, whose
name shall remain anonymous, had decided
to produce and post a video on the internet.
The whole production was an attempt to
showoff how he and his fellow gang bangers
were a "bad ass" group.*

*The group stood together showing off a
collection of firearms and rifles. The only
problem was that the gang banger and some
within his band of bandits were convicted
felons and thus in illegal possession of
the firearms. As a matter of fact, the gang
banger had multiple convictions which made
him eligible to be charged under Federal law.
In the end, the gang banger was convicted
and sentenced to 15 years in Federal Prison.*

In closing I don't mean for you to be paranoid about social media. My only hope is that you have become more aware of social media's darker side and perhaps it might inspire you to return to more personal interaction

Well, that's it for the burglary awareness and prevention chapter of this book. We have covered all of what I consider to be the most comprehensive list of topics that when put all together, or even taken in part, will decrease your chances of becoming a burglary victim.

Remember that alarm systems, video systems, storage of valuables, safes, pets, CPTED, structural barriers, Neighborhood Crime Watch, neighbors, having a plan and of course social media are all subject to what you make of them. It is my hope that I have provided you with enough information with which to make an educated decision about your home or business safety and security.

CHAPTER FIVE

HOME/BUSINESS INVENTORY

Detailed Inventory

A home or business inventory is one of the most important things you should have recorded. Many burglary victims struggle with reporting stolen property to the police and insurance companies alike. For this very reason I decided to include a guide of how, by taking just a short bit of time, you can save going through hours and days of angst and uncertainty. By following some simple steps, you can rest assured that you will have all of your valuables properly documented and marked for identification.

In the chapter, Should You Become a Victim, I write a segment about reporting what was stolen. In that segment I detail what will be expected of you to report to the responding officer, to include the make, model, serial numbers and more. Obviously, this will be a daunting task for someone who has just suffered a burglary. So, with this in mind we will attempt to relieve some of that stress by preparing you for what we hope never to occur.

In preparation of compiling a home/business inventory of your valuables, I suggest that you first contact your insurance company and verify what information and/or proof they require for a property loss claim. This will serve of value not only for the theft of property but as well for other types of loss such as fire, flood, etc. Once you have the insurance company requirements in hand you can begin your inventory. Let me note that depending on your insurance coverages or protocol, you may be required to have more documentation such as appraisal certificates. I will cover more about insurance in the following chapter.

To begin, I suggest you start your inventory utilizing a rough draft by topic such as jewelry, computers, TV, electronics, cameras, video games, cell phones and, of course, firearms. These are all of the more common items that I have seen reported stolen in countless burglary reports. As well, you would also include other valuables such as appliances, clothing and don't forget those designer handbags and shoes. Let's not forget any special equipment/electronics you may have in your vehicle.

Once you have put together that list, you can begin to fill in the blanks as to insurance requirements and what the responding officer will need for his/her police report. Police reports primarily focus on information required for identification of the property that has been stolen. This would include make, model, serial number, etc. The report also requires the value of the property. The value of the property determines the classification/degree of the theft (misdemeanor or 1st, 2nd, 3rd degree felony

The Miami-Dade Police Department provides a victim with a Property Loss Report, for the victim to complete and submit following the burglary. This gives the victim the chance to gather their thoughts and deal with the issue more calmly post burglary. I'm sure you can now begin to understand how your home/business inventory will alleviate much of this paperwork and stress. Let me emphasize that the most detailed section of the report will be that of jewelry which includes a bazillion (I'm exaggerating) examples of the type/shape of gemstones. In addition to description you will be asked to provide a karat weight and any other unique characteristics

Did you know that some diamonds have a serial number? Diamonds that have been graded by the Gemological Institute of America (GIA) as part of their certification process have a serial number applied by laser inscription. The inscription is applied to the girdle (outer edge) of the diamond. I don't know about you, but when I found out about this it blew my mind. Actually, some jewelers offer personalized wording lasered on the girdle of your diamond. One of those things you might want to look up.

Property Identification

As I mentioned, property identification is what the police department will focus on. It means everything to not only the successful recovery of the property but the successful prosecution of the burglar. Should you have followed the preceding steps and completed a detailed inventory you are going to make your detective very happy.

Once you have reported your property loss to the police department, if you provided a serial number, it will be entered in a law enforcement database. This way should an officer come upon some property that he/she suspects to be stolen and runs the serial number through the data base, bingo, it will come up as belonging to you. The officer will then attempt to contact you and/or your detective for follow-up.

Now let's take the area of property identification to another level. How can we assure property to be yours not only based upon make, model and serial number as you've reported? The answer is to place your own "mark" on the property in question. Perhaps you're wondering what kind of mark I am referring to. Well any marking (inscription) might work to set your property apart though what I would prefer is that, if at all possible, you inscribe your driver's license number on your property. You see, your driver's license number is unique to you just like your social security number. The difference being that you should never mark your property with your social security number to prevent against identity theft.

Now let's take the above example of a police officer coming upon some property that he/she suspects to have been stolen. As noted, the serial number will come up as stolen. Having a driver's license number is of even more value as it will serve as an instant means of contact for you. Driver's license records will have your address and phone contact information. And, in Florida even emergency contact information is included. All the more important for you to keep your driver license address and contact information up to date.

Not just a Number

Let me share a story with you that clearly expresses the value of this type of identification. One day my fellow detectives and I were conducting an enhanced enforcement initiative to combat burglary in a specific area of concern. In the course of this detail a vehicle was stopped, and a quantity of property was discovered in the trunk that would be considered atypical of what would commonly be taken in a residential burglary. We ran some of the serial numbers from the property to no avail. Mixed in with this property we came across some credit cards and a driver's license that did not belong to the driver or any of the occupants of the vehicle. When we queried the driver's license number, we were able to contact the owner. As it turned out the owner's residence had just been burglarized and we had the burglars and the stolen property all in one. In this particular case the burglars took the victim's credit cards and driver's license. We were able to make an arrest and recover the victim's property. Absent that driver's license, we would have had to release the subjects as we did not have enough probable cause to further detain them.

As you can tell from the above case, the result would have been the same if any of the property had been marked with the driver's license number for identification.

Finally, let me suggest that one of the best ways to mark your property would be with the use of an engraving tool. Engraving tools are sold in a number of stores and at a reasonable cost. Unlike a permanent marker or the like, the engraving tool will etch your mark into the material you are working with whether it be plastic, wood or metal.

Photography/Videography

In closing this chapter, let's discuss photography and videography as it pertains to your home/business inventory. As the saying goes, a picture is worth a thousand words. Photography is a means by which you will be able to enhance your inventory list. Photos and/or video taken of your property and home in general will go a long way in helping the police in the event of a burglary.

In many of the cases I investigated, victims provided me with photographs of themselves wearing a particular piece of jewelry. The only problem with that, was that the subject of the photo was the victim and not a closeup of the jewelry they were wearing. This made it difficult to use the photo for identification purposes. Granted, I did have something to go on although I would have loved to have had an actual photo of the jewelry alone.

To highlight how photographs of jewelry can be beneficial I need to tell you about bulletins. You see, when I was provided with what I will refer to as "photos of value" by a victim, I would have a stolen property bulletin published depicting the photos of the stolen jewelry. Of course, this worked as well for other stolen property of a unique nature whether it be a sculpture or perhaps a collectible. The bulletin would then be distributed across the department and even to outside agencies dependent on the circumstances. To put it simply, this was great for the investigation as I had the ability to advertise the case. Hundreds of officers and detectives are made aware of the property being sought.

Another benefit of photographs allows detectives to show them to local pawn shops. I cover pawn shops later in the book though my point here is that I could compare recent pawn transactions of jewelry against the photographs. I have been successful in doing this in the past and it made for the recovery of additional property that was linked to the photographed item.

My advice would be for you to photograph a closeup of all of the items in inventory and should you wish, take a video as well. When photographing each item, take the photo with the thought of being able to best identify that item. To accomplish this, you may want to take a number of photographs of the piece from a variety of angles. Don't worry about taking too many photos, just be sure you have an accurate depiction of the item. And of course, make sure to focus. Don't laugh. You'd be surprised what some people provide for identification.

CHAPTER SIX

*I*NSURANCE

I wanted to include a chapter on insurance as I have seen victim after victim of burglary realize, after the fact, that their coverages were not sufficient to cover the losses they had suffered. Imagine having to first deal with being the victim of a crime and then to learn that your insurance company will not cover the losses. For lack of other words, it's like a double whammy. It is the hope of every victim covered by insurance that the only concern or out of pocket expense would be that of the assigned deductible.

In the course of investigating cases, I was required to document the losses suffered by the victim. This was an important issue, both to assess the statutory degree of theft and/or damage (criminal mischief/ vandalism), and also to document what restitution the victim would be seeking in the criminal proceedings. Time and time again due to insufficient coverage, or no coverage at all, the only recourse a victim had was to hope for a court ordered restitution to recover the loss. The big little detail is you would be dependent on the defendant to pay the restitution as ordered.

With this in mind, in this chapter I will cover typical insurance coverages, optional/extended coverages referred to as insurance riders or scheduled personal property and required documentation to include appraisals

I want to note that I am not, nor have I ever been, a licensed insurance agent. Prior to making any decision concerning insurance coverages, you must thoroughly research what best fits the needs of your home or business. Therefore, I would suggest that you contact a qualified licensed insurance agent to assure you are properly covered.

Typical Coverage/Know Yours

In my experience the first time I considered homeowners insurance was when I purchased my first home. Homeowners insurance was just one of those things you automatically had to secure as part of the whole process of the purchase along with securing a mortgage and learning about principle, interest, taxes and insurance (PITI). My primary concern was that of the mortgage payment. Of course, I shopped around for insurance. My focus was on how much it was going to cost. The last thing I thought to consider was the fine print of the policy. More specifically, what were my specific coverages or limits should I become the victim of a theft or burglary. It was not until I became a police officer that I became aware of the importance of this issue.

Whether you own or rent a home, or own a business, it is important that you secure some form of insurance. I was surprised at the number of victims that did not have any coverage at all. The majority of those being renters. Many renters were not aware that insurance companies offered products for those who rent homes or apartments and at a very reasonable cost

A typical homeowners policy covers the dwelling for such things as fire, windstorms, lightning strikes, water damage, vandalism, etc. A typical policy will also cover some level of liability and personal property coverage. The personal property coverage is the section which covers your personal belongings and the section to focus on in the event of theft or burglary.

Personal property coverage will generally be broken down into two categories; replacement cost or cash value. Replacement cost policies replace damaged or stolen property at the value of that item when you file your claim. Cash value policies only pay you the value of the item minus depreciation.

> *The most important thing to know about personal property coverage is that the typical policy has limits on what an insurance company will pay you per item or category of items.*

As I noted, throughout my career I saw many victims of theft or burglary become crudely aware of their insurance coverage or lack thereof after the fact. Many victims were faced with unsurmountable losses as they learned that the insurance company had a limit on valuables such as jewelry, watches, art, antiques, stamp or coin collections and more. Most victims told me they were only able to recover a fraction of the value. The limit on jewelry was usually $1000.00 to $1500.00, in total and not per item.

Black Diamond Devastation

> *A case I handled that is probably the best example of insufficient coverage would be a residential burglary and grand theft of heirloom jewelry. The victim had a collection of black diamonds that had been handed down by her family over generations. The collection was said to be priceless. When I met with the victim she was absolutely devastated. I can still remember to this day how overwhelmed she was. What had been a priceless collection in her family for years was gone within minutes and the worst was yet to come. The victim contacted me several days following the burglary in tears as her insurance company had informed her that the limit on her heirloom black diamond collection was $1500.00. Not only was she distraught over the loss of her family's collection; now she had to deal with a financial loss that could have been easily averted with the proper insurance coverage.*

So, I suggest you review your current policy and verify your coverages. As you can see, it is important that you are familiar with your type of coverage and more importantly, the allowed limits.

Riders/Scheduled Personal Property Coverage

The resolve to insurance coverage limits would be to purchase scheduled personal property coverage, also referred to as an insurance rider. This coverage is optional to your policy and is specific to the item or items you wish to cover that are not covered in the primary policy.

Jewelry, watches, art, antiques, firearms, stamp or coin collections and even musical instruments are all examples of what can be covered by a separate insurance rider.

One of the other benefits of insurance riders is that they can cover accidental loss of your valuables and you may choose a lower/ higher deductible or no deductible at all. Of course, these benefits like everything in life, come at a cost.

Required Documentation/Appraisals

Now let's talk about required documentation and appraisals related to insurance. As a police officer, from day one in the police academy and throughout my career I learned documentation is everything. If it's not documented, it's as if it didn't exist or never happened. Applying this principle to that of your valuables for insurance is equally true.

Insurance companies generally require some form of documentation of your valuables in order to cover you in the event of a loss. This would commonly be in the form of receipts or the like. As I noted in the Home/Business Inventory chapter of this book, an inventory of your personal belongings and valuables is another important form of documentation. It is important for you to check with your insurance company to verify what specific documentation they require.

Insurance riders or scheduled personal property coverages generally require specific documentation above and beyond receipts to include an appraisal of the insured valuables. An appraisal is the value assigned to your property by a licensed appraiser based on its quality or importance. This is derived by a number of factors including market value or public opinion.

What is important to note about appraisals is that an appraisal is time sensitive. That is to say, the value of your property may fluctuate over time. So, it's important to keep an appraisal up to date with current market values. A good example of this principle would be to look at the gold market or that of diamonds. I'm sure you would find that an appraisal of a wedding band you purchased and appraised a number of years ago would now have a greater value. If you were to suffer a burglary/theft you surely would want to be insured for the current value in today's market.

The Insurance Information Institute

I want to close this chapter by mentioning the Insurance Information Institute (III.Org), a nonprofit organization founded in 1959. The III provides information for consumers about all types of insurance and related topics. It has helped me to better understand a multitude of insurance concerns and I found it to be a good resource for research. It might prove beneficial for you to check it out, too.

CHAPTER SEVEN

HAVING A GUN IN YOUR HOME OR BUSINESS

Gun Ownership

Having a gun in your home or business is probably the most challenging topic of this book. I use the word challenging because there are so many aspects of gun ownership ranging from criminal and civil liability, to proficiency, to the science of firing a weapon and beyond. In conjunction with gun ownership is responsibility, undoubtedly one of the most challenging responsibilities you will ever have.

It is imperative that you use this text only as a guide to conduct your own research and come to your own decisions and/or actions based on your particular situation and/or laws within the jurisdiction in which you reside or work.

Throughout my career, whether as a uniform patrol officer or as a detective, a multitude of people have asked me about firearms. Of course, one of the first questions was what firearm I carried on or off duty. The follow-up to that question would generally be what advice I could give concerning one aspect or another of firearm use. With concern to burglary, besides questions about alarm systems, the most popular question asked was, "What do you think about getting a gun for my home or business?"

As you know, the topic of firearms is a very heated and polarizing topic in this country. For those of you wondering what my personal thoughts about gun ownership or the second amendment of the United States Constitution are, let me emphatically state that I don't want my written words to be referenced as any type of moral or political statement. Just as I put my heart and soul into the creation of this book strictly for the benefit and well-being of others, I will only share that which I feel would help accomplish that intention. My wish is to inform and not to take any side, ideology or political stance.

It's important to mention that firearms are not only utilized for personal protection. Many people purchase and enjoy firearms for a multitude of uses to include hunting, target shooting and collecting to mention a few. My focus throughout this chapter will be to address what I believe to be the most important aspects of the ownership and use of a firearm as applied to your home or business.

In my experience, many victims of burglary who were not gun owners have expressed an interest in considering a firearm as part of their plan to protect themselves and their property. I believe this to be in large part due to the psychological effect and feelings of fear and angst they were now sensing as a result of being victimized. Many have said they felt that having a firearm would help bolster a feeling of security and safety.

Criminal and Civil Liability

Let me begin with what I believe to be the single most important factor of gun ownership, criminal and civil liability. Anyone who has made a decision to own or use a firearm must consider the accompanied criminal and civil liability that cannot be ignored. In the State of Florida, statutes cover a multitude of issues which must be adhered to. They range from; the justifiable use of force to protect one's self and home or personal property, safe storage of a firearm, proper carrying of a firearm, improper exhibition, discharging a firearm, use of a firearm while under the influence of alcohol/drugs, furnishing firearms to minors (under 18) or a person of unsound mind, and firearm ammunition to name a few

I would like to highlight the proper storage of guns. This is of serious concern as many innocent people are killed each year as a result of a firearm not having been appropriately secured. Florida is a state that covers the proper storage of a firearm by statute, Safe Storage of Firearm (FSS 790.174).

Quick Note

I have personally witnessed the tragic
result of a firearm having been left unattended
thus readily available to anyone. The case
was one in which a boy knew where his father
kept his gun. The boy had some friends at

I highly recommend that firearms be stored in a safe place. This could be in a locked drawer or gun safe. Not only stored but also properly secured, meaning that you have a trigger lock device. This way, even if the gun is found it would be incapable of being fired. I would refer to it as layered firearm security. This is especially important in households with children.

As I have mentioned burglars are known to take firearms. The proper storage of a firearm may prevent the burglar from stealing it or better yet, arming himself. Should you and/or a loved one interrupt a burglary in progress whereby the burglar has found your firearm lying around, the result could be catastrophic.

Cooling Off Period?

I investigated a residential burglary in which the victim's firearm (revolver) had been stolen. Fortunately, I was able to arrest the burglar within hours of the burglary. The burglar agreed to cooperate and told me where I could find the person to whom he had sold the gun. Given that the recovery of a gun is a high priority, I immediately contacted the buyer. The buyer told me that he had already sold the gun to a friend of his. To make a long story short, I pursued every lead. In the end, I recovered the gun after it had changed hands five times, all within 24 hours of its original theft. So much for a "cooling off period" or the like.

As you can see, gun storage can have a profound effect in many different ways. Something to consider.

In trying to equate criminal and civil liability to you, I'd like to mention that even law enforcement officers are not exempt and are faced with criminal and civil liability concerning the use of their firearm. Unlike what is often depicted in numerous television shows or movies in which the police shoot everything up and a few minutes later are on their merry way, officers face tremendous scrutiny when having fired their weapon.

Once an officer has decided to employ his/her firearm to combat a threat which he/she felt to be that of deadly force, he/she now becomes the subject of an investigation. That is to say, the officer's name will now appear as the one being investigated. Should the officer not have sustained any injury thus still on the scene, he/she will be isolated from the investigative process until such time as a formal statement be made, or not, when in the company of his/her attorney. In the meantime, a whole team of investigators to include those from the Homicide Bureau, Internal Affairs and State Attorney's Office will review every aspect of the shooting. The Crime Scene Unit would process the scene as well to include impounding the officer's firearm.

In the end, the investigation will assess whether or not the officer was criminally liable and whether or not Department policy and/or procedure was followed. Finally, a civil law suit may follow all of this to further challenge the offense/incident.

To put this into perspective for you, for using a firearm to defend yourself in the course of a burglary, you should expect to undergo some measure of scrutiny. Above and beyond you being the victim of a burglary, you will also be the subject of a criminal investigation concerning actions surrounding the use of your firearm. The police department and State Attorney's Office will now have to determine whether or not you were within your legal rights in the use of that firearm.

On the other side of the spectrum lies civil liability. Will you have to face a civil action filed by the burglar or the burglar's family? Criminal law with all of its statutes is totally separate and apart from a civil action. A civil action, more commonly referred to as a lawsuit, can be brought forth to dispute the action(s) you took to protect yourself and property regardless of the outcome of the criminal investigation. Criminal and civil law are independent of each other and carry a different burden of proof.

Quick Note

> *One example of criminal and civil liability would be to look at the infamous O.J. Simpson case. O.J. was charged with murder and criminally prosecuted for that crime. In the end he was found not guilty of the criminal charges. Following the criminal case, O.J. was then faced with a wrongful death suit in civil court for his actions. The result of the civil case ending in favor of the plaintiffs, the Goldman family and Brown estate.*

One thing you can be assured of when dealing with issues of criminal and civil liability is there are countless scenarios I could write about. The truth is that no two are exactly alike. Each and every "what if" has its own myriad of possible outcomes. So perhaps this gives you a chance to pause and reflect what would be best for you and of your family.

Buying a Gun

Now let's focus on the types of firearms you may be considering. This brings to mind the first time I went to a gun store. The salesman took out a number of pistols and proceeded to tell me what each firearm did ranging from revolvers to semi-automatic pistols. There were small guns to large ones, lightweight to heavy, some that carried only two bullets when fully loaded to those of fifteen bullets or more, and the caliber (inside diameter of the gun barrel and corresponding size of the bullet). I was a bit overwhelmed as there were so many factors to consider. I'm sure if you have ever been in a gun store you know exactly what I'm talking about.

In the end, I remember getting some sound advice from someone who wasn't interested in selling me a gun at all and just wanted to share some basic principles to consider. To this day I have found the advice to stand true. I was told to concentrate on only two things, comfort and reliability. Comfort, as it related to the fit of the gun in my hand. Having a firearm that is too large or small won't fit properly in your hand and may affect your ability to properly aim and hit a target. And reliability as in having confidence that the firearm would operate as expected. When considering the use of a semi-automatic pistol, versus a revolver, semi-automatic pistols may malfunction, experiencing what is commonly referred to as a misfeed or jam. Without proper training and practice on how to clear the firearm you could be placed in further danger. A revolver would be considered more basic in function and less likely to misfire and thus more reliable.

Firearm Proficiency

Should you already own a firearm or are considering purchasing one, you will need to be proficient in its use. To be proficient is to be competent and skilled. One way to help accomplish this is to attend a class at any number of gun stores. Notice I use the word help. That's because becoming proficient in the use of firearms goes beyond simply attending a class. I would ask that you know how to break the firearm down (take it apart); that you know how to properly clean the weapon so as to maintain it in proper working order, and of course, you need to know how to shoot your gun and what to do if it misfires.

The first rule of firearm proficiency is to always be SAFE. **Always handle a firearm as if it were loaded** and check if the weapon is clear, meaning be sure that all of the bullets have been unloaded from the firearm. When inspecting a revolver, verify that the cylinder has been emptied and there are no bullets remaining in any of the chambers. And when inspecting a semi-auto pistol, verify that not only has the magazine been removed though also that the chamber is empty. Many accidental discharges are a result of forgetting to check the chamber for a bullet.

When I became a police officer and was in the academy, I remember one of the most talked about subjects was firearms. I remember thinking we were all going to be just given a gun and walked out to the firearms range to practice shooting. Wrong! Instead, we sat in a classroom for countless hours learning about every aspect of shooting without firing the first bullet. We were taught everything from firearm safety to the nomenclature (parts) of the firearm we were about to be issued. When the day finally came to hit the range my fellow trainees and I were ready to go. But wait… more lecture. That's right, we were further instructed as to firearms range safety. This included how to properly carry a loaded firearm.

THE BIG DAY… After days and hours of instruction, the day finally came when we all got to shoot our newly issued firearm. And shoot we did! Over the next days we fired over 1000 rounds (bullets) of ammunition. The objective, to become proficient. There we were trying to attain proficiency to the best of our abilities. Not all of my fellow trainees were able to meet the mark and sadly they were terminated.

Anyway, getting back to the subject. What we underwent in the academy and then throughout years of continued training required by the Department, was to be and remain proficient. So likewise, I expect that you take as much time as you need to learn everything you can about owning/operating your firearm. Which leads me to the next step, muscle memory.

Muscle memory is that which you attain by repetitive action and committing those actions to your subconscious. To give you an example of this I will share another story.

In the course of firearms training we were trained to shoot at our targets and when out of bullets, reload as quickly as possible. This entailed dropping the spent shell casings, referred to as the "brass", from our revolvers (I'm dating myself) and reload with what we called speed loaders. After many rounds of practice, we would then have to clean up or "police" the brass from the firearms range.

We were told of a police officer that had lost his life in a gun battle with a subject due to the fact he did not have enough time to reload his firearm and face the oncoming threat which ended his life. You see, after running out of bullets, instead of immediately reloading as we had been trained to do, he paused to gather (police) his brass and stacked it neatly in a row. This was his fatal mistake. An investigation into why he would have paused to do such an odd thing instead of just reloading to return fire revealed something quite interesting.

As it turns out, when attending firearms training in the police academy, the officer was taught to "stack his brass" (placing the spent casings in a neat row) as it was found on the day of his death. You see the investigation thus concluded that the officer had resorted to what was "muscle memory" in his time of great stress.

So, as you can see given this example, it would be of the utmost importance to commit to some form of repetitive training and practice. It's important to understand that should you be faced with having to fire your weapon, you will be under stress and dependent on what you have trained for. Your training, proficiency and what you have committed to muscle memory can make the difference between life or death.

Firearm Science 101

Now that I have covered gun ownership, criminal/civil liability, buying a gun and firearm proficiency, the final topic to cover is what I refer to as firearm science 101. To accomplish this, I will be talking about firing a gun in your home or business environment, ammunition, bullet trajectory, and finally your ability to react to a threat. So, let's get started.

As you consider the use of a firearm as a means of protection in your home or business, you must consider the environment in which you would have to use (fire/discharge) the weapon. This would mean that you must now go beyond just aiming your weapon, what is commonly referred to as sight picture and be cognizant of your surroundings. Police officers are trained to not only face and engage a threat, though at the same time to evaluate the environment in which they may have to take action

First and foremost, one needs to be aware of others that may be in harm's way. When I speak of being aware of others who may be present, I am not just referring to those in the same room as you. On many occasions, dependent on trajectory (bullet path), bullets pass through walls which are commonly made of drywall, running the risk of striking a person in another room. The result could be devastating. I will cover this in a little more detail in a minute.

The lighting within your home or business is also an environmental factor to consider, especially in the darkness of night. It is imperative that you have the ability to clearly identify what you perceive to be a threat. You don't want to confuse the presence of a burglar with that of a loved one. It would be best to survey your home or business in the darkness of night and determine if there is enough ambient light. There are many lighting options available without having to have lamps or ceiling lights on.

A decision that you will be faced with, is the type of ammunition (bullet) to use. Again, there are a myriad of choices. There is a great deal of information available concerning different types of ammunition, much of which can be found on the internet. I would advise you to consider the design and power of the bullet as related to purpose and environment. When talking about personal or home protection, ideally you would want a bullet that serves to stop the threat and at the same time have a lower probability of passing through walls.

All bullets once fired from the barrel of a gun follow a certain trajectory (path) dependent on different environmental factors. Of course, you will be using the firearm within the close quarters of your home or business where factors such as distance and climate are not such a concern.

The concern of trajectory within the home or business is will the bullet stop after hitting it's intended target? Or will it continue through the target and strike another object or person? You will find that the design and power of the bullet has a great influence on the answers to these questions. Higher powered ammunition tends to travel at a higher velocity and greater distance than more conventional loads. In essence creating a higher likelihood that the bullet will strike a target and continue through that target and other barriers before reaching its final rest. This would be concerning for home and business environments.

A good example of trajectory to share with you, is one in which SWAT officers encountered an aggressive dog while serving a high-risk warrant. The dog charged one of the officers forcing him to fire on the dog in order to stop the threat of being bitten. The bullet passed through the dog into the ground and continued underground for some distance before resurfacing and striking another barrier above ground. Surely an astounding example of trajectory.

The most common firearm calibers for personal/home protection are 9mm and .38 caliber. I should note that there are various types of 9mm and .38 caliber bullets to choose from. Again, I would advise you to consult with a professional to become familiar with the various products available and which best suits your application.

Finally, let's talk about your ability to react to a threat. When addressing ability, I am talking about psychological ability and physiological ability. That is to say, your mental state of mind and your ability to physically function in a time of being faced with what you perceive to be a threat

When reflecting on many past experiences all sorts of human reactions come to mind. Whether calm or excited, being in fear or fearless, or not being able to react at all, I have seen many people, including police officers, react very differently when faced with a real-life threat as compared to one that has been imagined or trained for.

You can run through a number of scenarios in preparation of that moment when faced with real (live) danger and the use of a firearm, though never truly know how you will react based on psychological and/or physiological factors

Of great interest concerning this topic is having to deal with a threat upon waking. Should you awake in the middle of the night either by a sudden noise or your significant other shaking you and demanding you check the house. Been there, done that. You will of course need to gather your thoughts and take out your firearm.

Here's where it gets interesting. Let's assume that there is actually an intruder in your home. I think we can agree that the intruder will be wide awake and in a heightened state of mind and body given the adrenaline rush of breaking into a home he/she reasonably believes is occupied. Now here you come, armed and trying to gather your senses.

Let me introduce you to something called sleep inertia. Sleep inertia is known to occur upon being suddenly or abruptly woken. Effects of sleep inertia are grogginess, disorientation and cognitive/motor impairment. Sleep inertia typically lasts for fifteen to thirty minutes. Fifteen to thirty minutes when you may only have seconds to react to a threat. Do I have your attention?

As I was saying, here you come, armed, and trying to gather your senses or basically overcome sleep inertia. Putting aside the fact that you will be feeling groggy and somewhat disoriented, the critical issue will be the impairment of your cognitive and motor skills. Translation, you will experience diminished coordination between your eyes, hands and fingers. This obviously will put you at a great disadvantage in your ability to confront the intruder. Perhaps the better option would be to call for police assistance while remaining in place.

In closing the chapter on having a firearm in your home or business, some may think that my writings on this subject lean somewhat negatively regarding gun ownership. If you are one of those people, please understand that my hope is that whether you already own a firearm, are considering ownership or don't choose to own a firearm at all, my only wish is to spark a sense of awareness in your mind. As I have stated and repeatedly attempt to convey, it is through awareness that I believe one can make responsible decisions or at the very least be well informed. The fact is that historically, firearms have been a part of our culture and will continue to be present in our lives for good or bad. As I stated at the beginning of this chapter, the responsibility is ours.

CHAPTER EIGHT

*T*HINGS TO CONSIDER

In this chapter I wanted to talk about activities and/or interactions that may expose you to becoming a victim. Today in day, it is very common to open our homes to a number of people whether it be friends, visiting family or commercial services such as cleaning services or contractors. I have investigated many cases that ultimately led to the conclusion that some unsuspecting action or interaction of this nature was to the detriment of the victim. So, let me highlight some cases and present you with some tips that will help you avoid being victimized.

Having a Party?

So, you're having a party. This is probably one of the most common activities one opens his/her home to. We all love a good party. Usually this would entail you choosing a particular occasion and group of people to be attending. Anything from a small dinner party, to a full-blown invitation to all of your friends and family near and far to celebrate the occasion. Of course, there will be plenty of goodies such as food and yes, alcohol. Not to preach about the ills of alcohol, we just need to recognize that a drink or two does relax one's inhibitions and might tend to lead someone to do something, let's say, a bit out of the norm or outright illegal. Just a thought.

Now I don't expect you to conduct background checks and place security checkpoints around your home as if it were a White House dinner party. However, I would suggest that the setting of the party match that of the number of people attending. In essence, if you are having a small dinner party perhaps you can limit the space of the event to the den and dining room. In the case of a larger gathering, perhaps the outdoors (backyard) may serve well, weather permitting. The idea here is to isolate an area of your home for the event which will allow you to prepare that space to accommodate your guests.

Once you have selected your space you can now prepare the area for the gathering. By that I mean you can remove any and all articles of value, whether of monetary or sentimental value. It would behoove you to take the time to do a little redecorating in order to help avert a problem whether that problem be a theft or damage to personal property. I suggest you secure all valuables throughout the home. This would entail either locking a room to restrict access or locking your cash, jewelry and important documents in a safe or other secure area. In many cases subjects excuse themselves from the crowd with the common excuse of needing to use the restroom only to wander to, let's say the master bedroom, where you already have read is a prime target area for thieves.

Where's the Bathroom

As a side note having nothing to do with burglary, I remember as a child my parents had a party. As the party progressed into the night, I was cast off to my room at bedtime. There I was, lying in bed in the dark trying to sleep despite the noise of the party when this friend of my parents walked into my bedroom and opened my bedroom closet. This guy then proceeded to urinate in my bedroom closet. Once done, he closed the closet door and stumbled out of my room. I guess he thought he was in a bathroom or just really needed to relieve himself and didn't care where. Like I said, nothing to do with burglary.

Pretentious Display

So, let me close this segment with a story about a burglary victim who had a dinner party and decided to show off his collection of watches worth over $100,000.00. Someone at the party happened to mention having purchased a new watch. Seeing this as an opportunity to show his collection, *the victim eagerly escorted a select few individuals to where? You got it! The master bedroom. Picture it, these guests now stood there and observed where the victim stored and concealed his precious collection. You obviously know what happened later that week. The victim's home was burglarized, and the primary target of the burglary was the watch collection. As it turned out a distinguished guest had hired someone to burglarize the home and steal the collection. The moral of the story is that one should be careful not to reveal that which you would not want to be stolen.*

Children and Their Friends

I would have to say that the next most common nexus to exposing your home to a crime order problem is that of children and their friends. Now I don't mean to insinuate that all of your kids' friends are burglars. It's just important to know that a large number of burglaries are committed by juveniles. Some of which pick their victims via their relationships with other juveniles.

I Want to Be Your Friend

Case in point would be a burglary I investigated in which the victim's son had invited a friend from school to hang out with him at his home and check out his new gaming system. On its face, this was a quite normal and friendly interaction between kids with common interest in gaming.

The facts of the case were as follows; the burglary occurred sometime in the late afternoon, early evening hours of the day while the family was out and about. There was no forced entry. The point of entry was determined to be an unlocked sliding glass door at the rear of the residence. The only property taken was the gaming system in the victim's son's room along with various games and accessories. Upon speaking with the family, I was made aware of the noted visit that had taken place within a short time prior to the burglary.

Of course, the next step was to visit with the friend from school. Upon meeting with the young man, he immediately confessed to having stolen the game system and decided it would be better to cooperate and return the property he had taken than face other consequences. This worked to his advantage in his prosecution.

As it turned out, the school friend explained how he had not only committed this burglary though a handful of other burglaries of so called, "friends' homes". He told me that he had become accustomed to making friends with his fellow students with the intention of being invited to their home. Once inside, he had the opportunity to case the home and formulate a way to return and take what he wanted. His preferred method of entry was to enter via a door and/or window that he had unlocked during his earlier visit. This was simply accomplished by excusing himself for a bathroom break or being left alone at some point or another during the visit.

This is just one case in point where children visiting friends resulted in a burglary being committed. I investigated many cases wherein the common denominator was as result of juvenile interaction.

Now I know what you all must be thinking. Is he saying it's not a good idea for our children to have friends over? Not at all. A little bit of self-disclosure here. There were many times when my children had friends over and I understood that I couldn't restrict them from having visitors. My own parents always preferred me having friends over versus me wandering in the streets. The resolve to this situation was conversation with my children about what we often referred to as, our home and respect for each other's personal space.

Another key aspect of this principle was meeting with visiting friends. Of course, I refrained from going into what my wife referred to as cop mode. A simple introduction and light conversation made all the difference.

The final resolve was to agree to NO STRANGERS. Some might consider this a given requiring no discussion. I would strongly encourage you to define and discuss this principle. The word stranger by simple definition is a person who is unfamiliar. In the above case, the victim's son brought home a school friend who actually was a stranger. You see the son invited this boy whom he had just met at school and with whom he had not had any real interaction with. The victim's son was unfamiliar with his schoolmate.

In closing on this topic, I want to share a little story of when I was working Narcotics and assigned to a juvenile substance abuse task force. A mother called me one day about the arrest of her son for narcotics violations. She wanted me to tell her what she could do to resolve her situation with her son. Of course, my first thought was that if I had the answer to that question, I would be a very wealthy guy though I paused for a moment. It had become very clear to me that we live in such a difficult time where folks face so many challenges in raising children. In the end I told her to follow her heart and believe in her resolve. With that, I encourage all parents to do the same.

Cleaning Services

We all have read or seen crime dramas where the ending exclaimed, 'The butler (or the maid) did it'. Time and time again when investigating residential burglaries and thefts, whereby the victim employs a butler, maid or cleaning service, does the question arise whether the help had anything to do with it. Frankly I investigated only a few cases whereby the hired help was responsible or connected to the offense. Only because of the frequency of which the topic comes into question, I thought it prudent to include the topic in the book.

Today most cleaning services conduct background checks on its employees prior to hiring. This is of great importance to a company wishing to maintain a good reputation and lower its exposure to civil liability.

I have found that in most cases where the service was a subject of the investigation, it involved someone hired independently to clean. This would be perhaps someone, referred or not, who is less expensive and perhaps even paid on a cash basis and has not had their background checked. I understand trying to save money but my advice to you concerning this issue is to do your due diligence; check references, conduct a background check and conduct an in-depth interview. There are many companies that offer background checks at a reasonable cost.

Contractors

Contractors, for the purposes of the book, will include those you hire for purposes of repair, renovation or a complete build of your new home.

I would first like to address simple repairs such as air conditioning or plumbing. More than likely when you hire such contractors you will be at home while they are doing the repair. Just make sure that you are vigilant and if possible, present in the area where they are working. If you know in advance that you are either not able or don't wish to be watching over the work, perhaps you could follow the protocol for having folks come by for a party or visit. Make sure all of your valuables are secured. Remember if a theft were to occur in these circumstances it would more than likely be one of opportunity. This means that the setting was one that created the opportunity for the visitor to take advantage. Say you left your watch or ring out on the kitchen counter where the worker was working. He or she may feel tempted. Simply put, don't create temptation.

Next, we come to the renovation. This is pretty straight forward in that you will have planned in advance exactly what is entailed and know what areas of your home would be vulnerable to theft. The main difference here would be dealing with multiple workers given access to your home. Not to mention that some contractors would also be hiring sub-contractors to assist in the renovation.

Again, due diligence is the best course of action. When discussing design, price, etc., ask about staffing. Ask your contractor about what measures his or her company takes in order to ensure the people they have working with them are not only reliable to show up for work but also trustworthy. Perhaps the contractor's workers have been working for the company for a respectable time and have proven themselves. Along with checking proper licensing and insurance, also check with the Better Business Bureau and the governing agency in your area that licenses the contractor. Let's not forget the internet that can be a world of information with reviews of the contractors past jobs.

Quick Note

Regarding contractors, I would like to add that post Hurricane Andrew in 1992 Miami-Dade County had a serious problem with contractor fraud. One of my responsibilities was to liaison with the County's Contractor Fraud Investigators and effect the arrest of contractors which had violated contractor fraud laws. I strongly suggest you have

Again, I have highlighted these cases with the sole purpose of creating awareness. It is my hope that making you aware of what has occurred to others, helps you determine what action(s), if any, you may want to take in order to avoid becoming a victim.

CHAPTER NINE

IF YOU BECOME A VICTIM

As I started to formulate what areas of burglary were most important to make the reader aware of, I realized that I would be remiss not to consider that even if you followed every advice to prevent a burglary, you could still become a victim. As such, I wanted to include the most pertinent information should such an event occur. The following segments cover this area with both you and the officer/ detective assigned to the case.

Contacting the Police

Throughout my career both as a uniform officer and detective, I responded to thousands of calls for police assistance. Whether a routine call or that of an emergency, what I sometimes found frustrating was the victims' reaction or action following the offense/ incident. One's reaction or action more often than not could make or break a case, not to mention the possibility of placing oneself into further peril.

To be clear, I understand that many people react differently to a myriad of situations dependent on many different factors, at any given time. Of course, I don't want to appear here as if I didn't have any sort of sentiment for those concerned. It is specifically due to my concern for all involved that I wanted to address one's initial response.

First and foremost, immediately contact the police. Contacting the police seems to be a pretty straight forward initial response to any crime and I'm sure many of you think this is a no brainer. Why is he even writing about calling the police? As a matter of fact, many victims arriving home to discover that they have been burglarized, delay in contacting the police. Many victims walk through the residence amid a myriad of feelings and begin to check what had been taken and more than likely hinder the crime scene in doing so. I will address that in the next segment.

Be cautious. The burglar may still be in your home. You don't want to just walk about the house given the chance of a confrontation with the burglar. The moment you realize that you've been burglarized, walk back outside via the same route you entered while at the same time making a call for police assistance. This is the safest course of action.

As with any calls for police assistance, let's address the issue of emergency vs. non-emergency calls. Complaint officers taking the calls will first ask the question, 'What is your emergency? Based on your answer to this question the stage will be set for the type of response (emergency vs. routine) and what resources will be required.

When dealing with a burglary, the initial question is whether the burglary is in-progress or has it already been committed. Should it be the latter, then the response will be routine in nature. That doesn't mean that you should take your time in reporting the burglary. Time is always of the essence. The burglar(s) could still be in the area and still be in possession of your property. The sooner the police are made aware of the burglary and given the opportunity to gather important information i.e. a list of the property taken, witness testimony and any other evidence, the better chances are that an arrest could be made and/or your property recovered.

In the event of an in-progress burglary, the response will be much different. The complaint officer will remain on the telephone with you and walk you through a number of questions while a number of police units will be responding in a priority mode (lights/sirens). Of primary concern, will be that of your safety and well-being. It will be important to determine your location and that of the burglar. The burglar doesn't necessarily have to be inside your home. He/she may be at a door or window still attempting entry. You will be asked if you actually saw the burglar(s) and if so to provide a description. Given your response to these questions the complaint officer is trained to guide you pending the arrival of those units responding.

Finally, should you be in a situation whereby you need to; call 911 for assistance though can't speak for fear that the burglar may hear you; dial 911 in any case and leave the phone line open. Most police departments have systems in place to know where the call is coming from and have a mandatory response policy to investigate calls received with no caller acknowledgment.

Think Crime Scene

The crime scene is one of the most important and critical elements of a burglary investigation. Officers and detectives responding to your burglary will of course first be focused on safety for all concerned, beyond that their priority will be that of securing the crime scene. This will ensure that a crime lab technician will be able to conduct a proper search for evidence that has not been compromised or tainted.

As a side note, I should clarify that processing a burglary scene is much different from a homicide. Some of my victims had expected a team of crime scene investigators to appear and magically sweep the residence for the evidence that would enable detectives to make an arrest within hours. Sounds like a scene from some of your favorite TV shows. I can assure you that law enforcement will conduct a proper and complete investigation though resources dictate to what degree.

In order for a detective to be successful in solving your burglary, he/she must compile evidence from the crime scene. Evidence comes in many forms; though for purposes of a burglary investigation I will focus primarily on latent processing (fingerprints), DNA, and video surveillance footage.

Latent prints (fingerprints) are taken from items that the burglar handled though not all items are conducive to latent processing. Generally, latent prints are processed from items that have a smooth surface. Glass, metal or certain plastics to mention a few.

DNA (deoxyribonucleic acid) is now easily collected from a crime scene. This is accomplished by swabbing surfaces containing bodily fluids such as blood, urine or saliva. In many of my cases, burglars would cut themselves making entry through a broken window. Burglars would also take the opportunity to urinate and/or defecate in the residence and not always in a toilet. Also, believe it or not, some burglars are bold enough to treat themselves to a drink or meal. A DNA swab can also be taken from an object which the burglar handled with some degree of force usually leaving behind skin particles.

Video evidence is pretty self-explanatory. As I noted earlier in the book, this type of evidence is better recovered by a forensic video technician. Should you have a video surveillance system, I would suggest that you wait to review the video along with the detective and forensic technician. This would be especially true if you are not 100% familiar with your system. I frequently found this to be the case in many of my investigations.

So, taking all of the above into consideration, remember that should you arrive home and discover that you've been burglarized and the house has been ransacked, take a moment to think crime scene and refrain from taking any action that may hinder the investigation.

Reporting What Was Stolen

After the crime scene has been processed you will undoubtedly then begin to survey what has been stolen. The responding officer will be taking note of any items that you can readily account for. I say, readily account for, because you will obviously be upset and given the emotion, possibly not be able to account for all that has been taken. More often than not my victims would discover additional property that had been taken days or even weeks after. For this reason, we would provide victims with a Property Loss Report, which I covered in Home/Business Inventory, for use as a declaration of additional stolen property to be added to the original report.

A Bobcat You Say?

I had a case wherein the victim filed an initial report of approximately $1200.00 in stolen property consisting of jewelry, electronics and video games which at the time was pretty much the norm. I subsequently received a Property Loss Report declaring losses in excess of $65,000.00. Even more peculiar was that the additional items listed

My advice would be for you to have that inventory and identification documentation I previously noted in the Home/Business Inventory chapter of this book. This will relieve the stress of having to remember everything. It will act as a guide by having the corresponding serial numbers and/or your own identifying mark or number listed for the officer. Above and beyond filing a report, should you provide corresponding serial numbers of the stolen property, the officer will enter the numbers into a stolen property data base. This way any officer in the future running a routine record check on that property will be notified of its origin. I can't tell you how often officers stop subjects on routine traffic stops and come upon property in the vehicle believed to be stolen.

If it Quacks Like a Duck

Neighborhood Canvass

In Miami-Dade neighborhood canvassing is also a part of the responding officers' duties for the initial investigation and report of a burglary. The officer will go door to door in an attempt to contact any of your surrounding neighbors to gather possible leads for the detective. Many neighbors will often times see things that they dismiss as nothing of any importance though in fact were directly related to the burglary. This is specifically why I encourage folks to form neighborhood watch programs or at the very least, get to know your neighbor.

I have investigated many cases where a neighbor actually witnessed the burglary occurring though didn't think anything about it due to what I would call a lack of networking with neighbors. Networking with your neighbors is very important for many reasons though in some communities I have found that neighbors are like strangers to each other. If you think about it, we network with people all the time. In our jobs we are expected to network with others in order to be successful. So, I'm not expecting you to break bread or share your most intimate secrets with your neighbors, unless of course you're really feeling it; however, you can at least get to know each other by name and engage in casual conversation.

I would suggest you do whatever possible at the time of the initial report to contact your neighbors to see if they saw anything unusual. Remember time is of the essence and contacting neighbors (possible witnesses) as early as possible following the event can make a difference. Also, should you have the contact information for your neighbors, you could share that with the officer or detective.

Pawn Shops and Second-Hand Dealers

Over the years many victims would ask about whether or not they should check area pawn shops and/or second-hand dealers for their stolen property. Granted, many burglars do sell the property they have stolen to pawn shops, second-hand dealers, flea markets or simply on the street. Anyway, what you should know prior to running around town in search of your property, is that there are laws that govern how pawn shops and second-hand dealers operate. I would suggest that you first research the governing laws and regulations within your jurisdiction.

Florida for example has a law that is referred to as The Florida Pawnbroking Act (FSS 539.001). The Act, as I will refer to it, is very specific in outlining the responsibilities of the pawn broker when receiving property from an individual whether it be a pawn or purchase transaction. I will cover the sections of the Act that I believe relate to what the victim of a burglary should be aware of. I should also mention that I was given the responsibility of conducting pawn shop checks for a period of my career as a burglary detective. Of course, this played hand in hand with many of my investigations.

First, the Act requires that a pawn broker conducting a pawn or purchase transaction must secure the property for a period of 30 days. So, given this alone you see it would be a futile effort for you to run out looking for your stolen property. Most pawn shops will keep the property in a safe pending the 30-day time period, prior to placing it on display for sale or in the case of some jewelry, sending it off to be melted.

I'm sure you're asking yourself how is it then that anyone will know where my property has gone if it's locked up in some safe and then shipped off somewhere? Well another very important part of the Act is the Pawnbroker Transaction Form. This is the document, required by law, to be completed in detail for all pawn and purchase transactions. Let me outline what I like best about the document. It contains the type of identification presented, name, address, telephone number, place of employment, date of birth, physical description, and right thumbprint of the person conducting the transaction. Notice I have highlighted thumbprint. This is key as it will be a form of positive identification of the burglar or person related to the burglar conducting the transaction.

As to the listing of the concerned property, the law requires that the pawn broker give an accurate description to include; brand, model number, manufacturer's serial number, size, color, precious metal type, weight (content), and gemstone description (including number of stones). Firearms require the type of action, caliber or gauge, number of barrels, barrel length and finish. As well, include any other unique identifying marks, numbers, names or letters. Again, I'm highlighting this as it ties into what I covered in the Property Identification segment of the book. This will make it easy to prove ownership and what could be considered beyond any reasonable doubt.

The Act requires that the form be delivered to the law enforcement agency having jurisdiction by the day that follows the transaction. Let me point out that much of this is done electronically by computer. Awesome, right?

So finally, let's say a records search of the pawn data system reveals some articles listed on a pawn transaction form that appear to match your property. Your detective would personally visit the pawn shop and take a first-hand look at the property in an effort to make a positive identification. Should items match, that identity, the Act allows me to place a "hold" on the property for a period of 90 days. This allows time for further investigation of the transaction and possibly the arrest of the subject who committed the burglary.

You're probably wondering why I don't just bring the property back to you. The answer is that, according to the Act, the pawn broker still has at stake money that he/she paid the subject as well. You see, the law not only protects you, but the business interest of the pawn broker as long as all of the rules were followed. One way to resolve this issue is the victim has the right to "buy back" the property from the pawn broker for the exact amount that the broker purchased it. I know this sounds a bit crazy; but it's about trying to protect the pawn brokers rights as well. Now should an arrest be made, the money you paid to recover your property can be recovered as restitution if so ordered by the court.

The Prosecution Process

The prosecution is a process that will follow the arrest of the individual or individuals that are believed to be responsible for having committed your burglary. This process can be a long and arduous process, especially if you are not familiar with the criminal justice system.

I should explain that in the course of an investigation, the detective seeks to gather enough evidence to establish what is referred to as probable cause for the arrest of the individual(s) believed to be responsible for the burglary. Probable cause is built on facts, not mere suspicion, born from the investigation. This could be as result of crime scene evidence and/or witness testimony and/or finding of any other fact(s). The State has the "burden of proof" in criminal prosecutions to bring forth evidence that would prove the charges beyond any reasonable doubt.

Once the detective makes an arrest, you will be notified and expected to appear before an Assistant State Attorney. Remember to verify these steps within your jurisdiction though besides some minor differences, it should be more or less the same. In Miami-Dade this was referred to as a Pre-File Conference. This will be a brief informal meeting between you and the Assistant State Attorney and perhaps your detective as well. The purpose of the meeting will be to confirm the facts of the case and to review the process to come. After the Assistant State Attorney has reviewed the facts of the case, a determination will be made as to whether or not the State wishes to file the case, which would mean to pursue the prosecution of the individual(s) arrested.

Once the case has been filed by the State, the detective will eventually be deposed by the subject's defense attorney. You may or may not be deposed. No need to worry as the State will more than likely help you and be present through the process. This gives the defense attorney the opportunity to review what led to the arrest and charges filed against his/ her client. The defense attorney will also now be prepared to discuss the findings with the State.

As both the Assistant State Attorney and defense attorney discuss the case, a plea could be offered. A plea is basically an offer made to resolve the case without having to go to trial. The plea could involve jail/prison time, probation or both. More importantly for you is to make sure you are reimbursed for any losses in the form of court ordered restitution. It will be up to you to make sure that the State knows how you feel and what will make you whole. Remember, most prosecuting and defense attorneys are going to be treating the case as currently designated, a property crime. It will be up to you to let your feelings be known. The extent to which you and your family were personally affected. This will help in the plea process and help bring a sense of validation and help in the healing process of overcoming this personal crime.

Should the case go to court the State will assist you again in preparation of your testimony. Many victims are nervous about this step. Please don't worry about it. Victim testimony in burglary cases is pretty generic. By that I mean, unless you actually had a confrontation or something of the like with the burglar, you would only be there to verify that you don't know the defendant and did not give he/she permission to enter your home/business and remove your property. The officers, crime scene investigator and witnesses will have more time on the witness stand than you.

So, all in all I hope this basic explanation of the process can help you feel more at ease. Again, the reason I decided to cover this in the book is because of the number of victims who voiced angst over the prospect of having to go to court. In the end, most realized it wasn't half as bad as they had imagined.

One last thing to mention. Many victims expressed a feeling of fear that should they pursue a case, the defendant(s) would seek some type of retribution. I can tell you that over all of my twenty-nine-year law enforcement career, I never had a burglary victim harassed and/or harmed by the defendant(s) for pursuing a case. Frankly, I think much of this fear is generated from television and movies.

The Aftermath

As previously mentioned in my introduction, in its wake, burglary has left victims with feelings of having been violated. A crime causing its victims to no longer feel safe in their own home. And the children… My heart goes out to the many children that are literally terrified when they are confronted by a burglar that has forcefully entered the home.

Thinking that a stranger (criminal) has entered your home, your personal space, the place where you always felt secure is quite unnerving. It's not just about the theft or damage to your property, it's much deeper than that. This person has riffled through and physically touched your most personal possessions and clothing. Victims spoke of having to wash and sanitize everything in the home; sometimes even throwing away certain items because they couldn't bear the thought of it having been handled by this stranger.

With all of this in mind I wanted to share some thoughts and suggestions of what may serve you and your family well in the wake of this crime. Of course, I am not a psychologist or health care specialist. The advice that I offer you is merely based on the countless conversations with burglary victims and what they shared with me to be the most effective prescription for recovery from this crime. Above all, I believe that you must trust your own feelings as to what is appropriate for you and your family. There are avenues to explore for emotional help: state agencies and private counselors among them.

Many victims were selective as to whether or not they chose to share that a burglary had occurred in their home with other family members. I'm talking about minor children who were not present during or immediately following the burglary. Parents felt it better not to reveal what had occurred as a means of avoiding any negative feelings the knowledge thereof would bring. Again, this is a personal choice for you to consider given your instincts.

First, you need to talk about it. Conversation is a means by which you and your family can share any and all feelings about what occurred. The conversation should be one with the family seated all together and without distraction. And by distraction, I'm not only talking about the television. Collect everyone's cell phone, mute the volume and don't return them until the conversation has finished. You might actually enjoy this and do it more often in the future. Also, you may want to establish some ground rules. I remember growing up in a family of five children with ages spanning thirteen years apart. This made for quite a ruckus. Everyone should have the opportunity to speak freely, without interruption, and most of all, with no fear of negative feedback from anyone. All expressed feelings are welcomed.

As the conversation progresses, you should listen for certain words or phrases which may warrant further inquiry. In other words, someone in the family may be hesitant to reveal all of what they are feeling so they may talk in what I call rhymes and avoid answering the question all together. This sometimes signifies inner struggle.

Another means to encourage your family to express themselves is through self-disclosure. Self-disclosure is a process by which you reveal your feelings on the subject to invoke a response from another. As a hostage negotiator, I used self-disclosure quite often and with great success. It lets the person you're having a conversation with feel as if they are not the only one going through a particular situation. You will soon establish that you share certain feelings and are thus in it together to some degree.

Let me not dismiss the option of seeking professional guidance from a professional counselor such as a family psychologist or the like. Many victims told me they had sought counseling both individually and as a family. It is vital to seek professional help if one's feelings in the aftermath include deep despair, disillusionment, despondency, violation, or anger. Be aware that these feelings are very normal and perhaps to be expected given this crime is so very personal. I encourage all victims to seriously contemplate seeking professional counsel. It can and will help you deal with this offense.

As a final thought, enacting changes to your home after the crime would be recommended. This could be anything from adding some security measure such as an alarm system or impact resistant windows, to taking the family on a trip to the local animal rescue to adopt a puppy. The idea here is to put in place a symbol of what is now going to represent positive change that will stop the burglary from happening again. This tends to be especially successful with helping children overcome fears of the burglar returning to the home. The physical change of environment is reassuring in itself.

As I come to the end of this book it is only a part of a journey that is far from over. A journey that began with a small boy playing with toy police cars. A boy who remembers how one day after getting out of grade school he sat outside with all of the other students waiting to be picked up only to realize no one had come for him.

As he sat alone on a cement bench with no one around he wondered why no one had come for him. Then, to his surprise a police officer drove up in his patrol car and asked why he was sitting all alone. The boy answered that he was waiting for his mom to pick him up. The police officer told the boy to jump into his patrol car and he would give him a ride home. The boy eagerly accepted this offer to ride with the officer. This was no toy. Along the way the officer showed the boy how the lights and siren worked, as well as the police radio as he radioed into the police dispatch. The boy sat in amazement as he enjoyed each and every moment of the ride and thus forgetting all about the fear of abandonment, he had felt only moments ago.

Once the ride had come to an end, the boy realized that it was only the beginning as he would aspire to be just like that officer. That boy was me.

I would like to express that I feel blessed to have not only realized my dream to become a police officer though to have the opportunity to continue to serve my fellow citizens. Should this book help the life of only one person, I will believe it a success.

I'm reminded of how many times throughout my career I wondered if I was truly making a difference. I hadn't come along any boys sitting on a cold cement bench waiting for a ride home. Then one day as I was having lunch with my fellow officers, a woman approached me and excused herself for interrupting. She asked me if by any chance I remembered who she was. I didn't recognize her, and she then reminded me that I had once arrested her when she was a teenager for possession of LSD. She explained how she never forgot some words of wisdom that I had shared with her at the time. She wanted me to know that she had taken those words to heart and had straightened out her life. Now as a grown woman, married and the mother of two beautiful children. She then thanked me.

I can't tell you the impact that had on me; other than to say that it was at that moment I knew that I would never have to wonder again in my life if I had, or ever would make a difference.

Thank you for taking the time to read this book. I would ask that you continue to partner with me so that together we will be able to use this knowledge to effect change for you and generations to come and of course, **change the face of this very personal crime.**

TRAINING / CERTIFICATIONS

February 1986, Basic Law Enforcement Certificate, Miami-Dade Community College, Miami, Florida

November 1987, Alternatives to the Use of Force, Metropolitan Police Institute, Dade County, Florida

March 1988, Basic Semi-Automatic Pistol Course, Metropolitan Police Institute, Dade County, Florida

April 1988, Narcotics Identification and Investigation, Institute of Police Technology and Management, University of North Florida / Advanced Training Certificate, State of Florida Commission on Criminal Justice Standards and Training

February 1989, Search and Arrest Tactics for Narcotics Officers, Metropolitan Police Institute, Dade County, Florida

April 1989, Interview and Interrogation Techniques, Metropolitan Police Institute, Dade County Florida / Advanced Training Certificate, State of Florida Commission on Criminal Justice Standards and Training

May 1989, Crack Enforcement Training, Broward Sheriff's Office Organized Crime Centre, Broward County, Florida

June 1989, Two Week Law Enforcement Training School, United States Department of Justice, Drug Enforcement Administration, Ft. Myers, Florida

November 1989, Field Training Officer, Metropolitan Police Institute, Dade County Florida / Advanced Training Certificate, State of Florida Commission on Criminal Justice Standards and Training

May 1990, Semi-Automatic Transitional Training, Metropolitan Police Institute, Dade County Florida

November 1990, Field Training Officer Update, Metropolitan Police Institute, Dade County, Florida

February 1991, Mobile Field Force Training, Metropolitan Police Institute, Dade County, Florida

February 1991, Field Training Officer Update, Metropolitan Police Institute, Dade County, Florida

August 1991, Search Warrants, Metropolitan Police Institute, Dade County, Florida

September 1991, General Criminal Investigations, Metropolitan Police Institute, Dade County, Florida

October 1991, Robbery Intervention Detail, Metropolitan Police Institute, Dade County, Florida

November 1991, Field Training Officer Update, Metropolitan Police Institute, Dade County, Florida

January 1994, Mobile Field Force Specialized Course, Santa Fe Community College Institute of Public Safety, Gainesville, Florida

May 1994, Evidence Technician, City of Gainesville Police Department, Gainesville, Florida

September 1994, Instructor Techniques, Santa Fe Community College Institute of Public Safety, Gainesville, Florida / Instructor Certification, State of Florida Commission on Criminal Justice Standards and Training

June 1996, Police Driving Instructor, Santa Fe Community College Institute of Public Safety, Gainesville, Florida

June 1997, Hostage Negotiations, Santa Fe Community College Institute of Public Safety, Gainesville, Florida / Advanced Training Certificate, State of Florida Commission on Criminal Justice Standards and Training

June 1997, Human Diversity Instructor, Santa Fe Community College Institute of Public Safety, Gainesville, Florida

February/March 2000, Crisis Negotiation School, Jacksonville Sheriff's Office, Jacksonville, Florida In Cooperation with the Federal Bureau of Investigation

May 2000, Introduction to Community Policing, St. Petersburg Junior College, Florida Regional Community Policing Institute

July 2000, Problem Solving for the Community Policing Officer and Citizen, St. Petersburg Junior College, Florida Regional Community Policing Institute

October 2000, Police Community Partnerships, St. Petersburg Junior College, Florida Regional Community Policing Institute

May 2001, Lateral Entry Training Program, Metropolitan Police Institute, Miami-Dade County, Florida

September 2001, Verbal Judo for Field Training Officers/Supervisors, Metropolitan Police Institute, Miami-Dade County, Florida

September 2001, Field Training Officer/Supervisor Workshop, Metropolitan Police Institute, Miami-Dade County, Florida

November 2001, Chemical Agent Response Team, Metropolitan Police Institute, Miami-Dade County, Florida

March 2002, Professional Traffic Stops, Metropolitan Police Institute, Miami-Dade County, Florida

April 2002, C.P.R. & A.E.D. Instructors Course, Metropolitan Police Institute, Miami-Dade County, Florida

April 2002, D.O.T. First Responder Instructors Course, Metropolitan Police Institute, Miami-Dade County, Florida

April 2002, Human Diversity, Metropolitan Police Institute, Miami-Dade County, Florida

April 2002, Weapons of Mass Destruction, Metropolitan Police Institute, Miami-Dade County, Florida

April 2002, Incident Command Systems, Metropolitan Police Institute, Miami-Dade County, Florida

May 2002, FCIC Certification, Florida Department of Law Enforcement, Criminal Justice Information Services

August 2002, Special Events Response Team, Metropolitan Police Institute, Miami-Dade County, Florida

June 2003, Introduction to Community Policing / Managing Encounters with the Mentally Ill, St. Petersburg College Florida Regional Community Policing Institute

June 2003, Hostage Negotiator Certificate, Hostage Negotiation and Crisis Management facilitated by Division 18, Psychologists in Public Service, Police & Public Safety Psychology Section of the American Psychological Association.

February 2004, CMS Law Enforcement Vehicle Operations Instructor Transition, Miami-Dade College North Campus School of Justice, Miami-Dade, Florida

July 2004, Anti-Terrorist Concepts for the Patrol Officer and Supervisor, Sovereign Executive Services in association with the Miami-Dade Police Department

April 2006, Human Diversity and Professional Traffic Stops, Metropolitan Police Institute, Miami-Dade County, Florida

October 2006, Special Response Team Dignitary Protection Training, Miami-Dade Police Department Tactical Operations Section, Special Response Team

October 2006, Homeland Security and Terrorism, Metropolitan Police Institute, Miami-Dade County, Florida

June 2010, Police Urban Rifle Course, Miami-Dade Public Safety Training Institute, Miami-Dade County, Florida

August 2010, Managing Encounters with the Mentally Ill & Elder Abuse Investigations, Miami-Dade Public Safety Training Institute

June 2011, Domestic Terrorism Law Enforcement Training, FBI Miami South Florida Joint Terrorism Task Force

November 1987, Officer of the Month, Kiwanis Club of Perrine-Cutler Ridge, Miami, Florida

January 1988, Officer of the Month, Kiwanis Club of Perrine-Cutler Ridge, Miami, Florida

December 1988, Officer of the Month, Kiwanis Club of Perrine-Cutler Ridge, Miami, Florida

June 1991, Hispanic Officer of the Month, Hispanic Police Officers Association

August 1992, Officer of the Month, Miami-Dade Police Department Kendall Station

August 1992, Recognition of Outstanding Performance of Duties, The Elks Club, Miami-Dade County, Florida

November 1992, Exceptional Dedication and Outstanding Performance, The Citizens Advisory Committee of the Miami-Dade Police Kendall Station

1996-97, Certificate of Appreciation for Outstanding Contribution, Florida Law Enforcement Games

April-November 1999, Certificate of Appreciation, Police Community Committee, City of Gainesville, Florida

May 2002, Certificate of Commendation, Miami-Dade Police Department

October 2002, Certificate of Commendation, Miami-Dade Police Department

June 2003, Officer of the Month, Miami-Dade Police Department Kendall District

June 2003, Recognition of Outstanding Performance of Duties, The Elks Club, Miami-Dade County, Florida

June 2003, Distinguished Service Citation, Miami Sundown Rotary Club, Miami Florida

December 2003, Certificate of Commendation, Miami-Dade Police Department

June 2004, Employee Excellence Award, Miami-Dade Police Department

July 2004, Certificate of Commendation, Miami-Dade Police Department

July-September 2004, Unit of the Quarter, Miami-Dade Police Kendall District, General Investigations Burglary Squad

October 2005, Officer of the Month, Miami-Dade Police Kendall District

October 2005, Distinguished Service Citation, Miami Sundown Rotary Club, Miami Florida

January 2006, Certificate of Commendation, Miami-Dade Police Department

October 2007, Certificate of Commendation, Miami-Dade Police Department

2007, Officer of the Year, Miami-Dade Police Department Kendall District

April 2008, Certificate of Appreciation, Florida House of Representatives

January 2010, Certificate of Commendation, Miami-Dade Police Department

June 2011, Employee Excellence Award, Miami-Dade Police Department

May 2013, Certificate of Appreciation, Florida Department of Juvenile Justice

January 2014, Certificate of Commendation, Miami-Dade Police Department

July-September 2014, Officer of the Quarter, Town of Cutler Bay Policing Unit, Cutler Bay, Florida

Additionally, over 100 career citations/commendations from citizens, businesses and other law enforcement or government agencies.

Notes

Notes

Notes

Notes